PLAS

PITT
LATIN
AMERICAN
SERIES

Adventurers and Proletarians

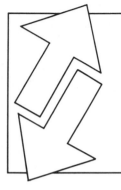

Adventurers and Proletarians
The Story of Migrants in Latin America

Magnus Mörner
with the collaboration of
Harold Sims

University of Pittsburgh Press

UNESCO, Paris

First published 1985
by the United Nations Educational, Scientific and Cultural Organization
7 Place de Fontenoy, Paris, France
and
University of Pittsburgh Press
127 N. Bellefield Avenue
Pittsburgh, PA 15260

Based on an original Spanish text
Culturas inmigratorias en America Latina
© UNESCO 1977

Revised and translated into English with the
financial assistance of UNESCO

© 1985 University of Pittsburgh Press
Feffer and Simons, Inc., London
Manufactured in the United States of America

Library of Congress Cataloging in Publication Data

Mörner, Magnus.
  Adventurers and poletarians.

  (Pitt Latin American series)
  Bibliography: p. 149.
  Includes index.
  1. Latin American—Emigration and immigration—History.
  2. Migration, Internal—Latin America—History.
  3. Assimilation (Sociology)—History. I. Sims, Harold.
II. Title. III. Series.
JV7398.M66 1985   325.8   84-19597
ISBN 0-8229-3505-8

Figures 12 and 15 and maps 1 and 2 are reprinted, with permission, from Magnus
Mörner, "Massutvandring över havet," *Vandrarsläktet Manniskan* (Stockholm:
Stiftelsen Forskning och Framsteg, 1982), p. 31, with special thanks to the artist, Ms.
Gunilla Kvarnström. Map 4, from Rosemary D. F. Bromley and R. Bromley, *South
American Development: A Geographical Introduction* (Cambridge: Cambridge
University Press, 1982), p. 78. is also reprinted with permission.

This book is dedicated to my former colleagues in the Department of History of the University of Pittsburgh, an exceptionally dynamic and stimulating intellectual environment.

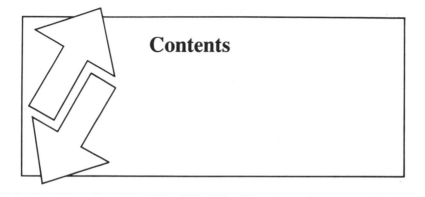

Contents

Tables and Illustrations

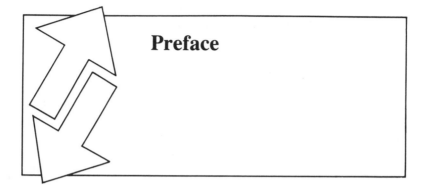

Preface

This little book has its origin in a commission received from UNESCO in the mid-1970s to write a historical introductory chapter for a collective work being planned and to be called "America Latina: Culturas Inmigratorias." I carried out the research and duly delivered a 100-page survey, written in Spanish to the UNESCO representative in early 1977. Simultaneously, at my suggestion, two graduate students at the University of Pittsburgh, where from 1976 until 1981 I held the Andrew W. Mellon chair in history, were equally commissioned by UNESCO to carry out an inventory of statistical source material relevant to the study. They were George Calafut, later a computer specialist, and Laird Bergad, now on the faculty of Herbert W. Lehman College, City University of New York.

UNESCO has so far only published a very small part of my report as an article in the multilingual *Cultures* review. Since 1976, evidently, research on the vast topic of migration to and within Latin America has advanced considerably. At the same time, surprisingly, to my knowledge there is still no general survey in English of the type attempted here. In the intervening years, with the invaluable help of my Pittsburgh colleague and friend, Harold Sims, I have tried to keep up with the rapid developments in historical and social science research. Although I left Pittsburgh in 1981, Professor Sims took care of the translation of the original report. In the course of this tedious and time-consuming work he also made many important revisions and additions to the text, only a few of which have been explicitly acknowledged in the notes. It should be pointed out, in particular, that most of what is now chapter 7 was, in fact, written by him. My debt to Professor Sims is, of course, only the most important one to be recognized here. I am also most obliged to his wife, Retsuko Sims, for her invaluable assistance in drawing the figures with the help of the computer. The work carried out by George Calafut and Laird Bergad has also been of great importance to the final product. I am also very grateful to my wife, and to my Swedish friend and fellow Latin American historian, Roland Anrup, for their constructive criticism of my manuscript.

Habent sua fata libelli, or "Books have their own adventures," is very appropriate here. Instead of explaining why this book did not appear before, let me simply make my acknowledgments where they are due. First, despite all the problems involved, I think UNESCO deserves some praise for having made me take on this fascinating though arduous task. Also their permission to publish this considerably updated and, I hope, improved version of the original report is duly acknowledged. At the same time, it must be noted that UNESCO laid claim to all the royalties accruing from the present book. As the author, it only remains for me to wish that the monies be used wisely.

With respect to editorial work, let me give my thanks to Mr. J. Armesto, of the UNESCO staff, for his assistance with the final version and, in particular, to Ms. Jane Flanders, of the University of Pittsburgh Press, who edited it in an exemplary manner. More than most short surveys, this one required often difficult and time-consuming research in a great variety of literature in many languages. Under these circumstances I have caused much trouble for the personnel of the various libraries where I have worked. I gratefully acknowledge the help of the following:

Institute of Latin American Studies, Stockholm;
The Hillman Library, University of Pittsburgh;
Iberoamerikanisches Institut, West Berlin;
The Library of Congress, Hispanic Foundation, Washington, D.C.;
The Nettie Lee Benson Latin American Collection, University of
Texas.

The final revision of the manuscript was undertaken at the last-mentioned university in the course of a two-month stay as a visiting professor in early 1983, which gave me an excellent opportunity to complete my work.

Last but not least, let me express more than the usual debt of gratitude to the editors of the University of Pittsburgh Press for their patience, understanding, and helpfulness throughout the lengthy "gestation" of this book.

Göteborg, Sweden
March 1983

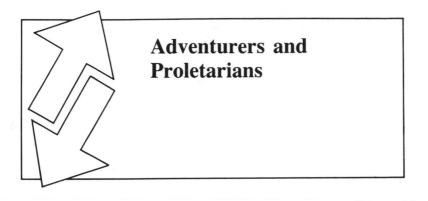

Adventurers and Proletarians

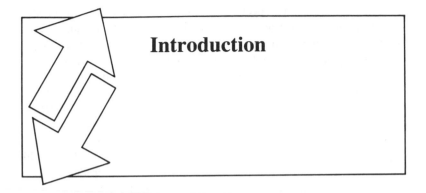

Introduction

As far back as historians and even archaeologists are able to see through the mists of the past, scattered individuals with or without their families, as well as large groups of people, were very often on the move. At times their destinations must have been clearly defined, especially as far as shorter distances were concerned. In other cases migrants seem to have aimlessly drifted along in quest of better conditions for survival.

Concerning the remote past, such movements are hard for us to pin down. Often they can only be presumed to have taken place from abrupt changes in cultural patterns such as in burial customs or types of tools and arms. The early accounts of movements of tribes more often than not blend with legend and myth around cultural heroes. And, with conspicuous exceptions such as the Mongol invasions of Europe or the Western crusades, movement usually covered only short distances or were extremely slow, stretching over many generations, such as those of the Celtic, Germanic, and Slavonic tribes. From the Age of Discovery (to use an admittedly ethnocentric concept) onward, the mass movement of peoples took on a new dimension, facilitated by steadily improving transportation and spurred by the drive of the new European states to establish overseas colonies. Thus European immigration was superimposed on native populations or, in fact, replaced them to become the basis for the formation of new societies built on the European model. This happened in the Americas, Australia, South Africa, and a great number of lesser territories scattered around the world. Yet, from a longer time perspective, even these movements of people remained rather modest in both relative and absolute terms until recent centuries. Transportation was slow, costly, and often dangerous. Also, only a small part of the European masses were willing to change even a meager livelihood in the homeland for a presumably better life overseas. Thus the forced transportation of black slaves and indentured labor formed a large proportion of those crossing the Atlantic in one direction or another. Only toward the mid-nineteenth century did the era of real mass migration begin, induced by European population growth, vastly improved and cheaper transportation, and the formation of a world market strictly divided between industrial and primary producers. Initially, migrants hoped to find work as producers of foodstuffs or other necessities for Europe, which was already in the midst of industrialization. Thus, the bulk of mass migration took place between 1850 and 1930, when the world market collapsed with the onset of the Great Depression. Our main attention in this book will be given to Latin America's part in this worldwide phenomenon, because the impact of immigration in demographic and social terms was absolutely fundamental in parts of Latin America such as Argentina and Uruguay, in the south of Chile and Brazil, and in Cuba. But we shall also try to outline more recent developments characterized by the outflow of Latin Americans to other—and, from their point of view, more promising—parts of the world, and to discuss in brief the massive migrations taking place within Latin America itself.

In order to treat vast and complex themes with brevity, as we attempt to do, we must establish strict definitions of concepts from the outset. *Migration* implies a spatial movement with lasting objectives and results. People who migrate have made a decision as a consequence of a comparative evaluation between their situation in the place of origin and a hoped-for situation in the place of destination.[1] Migration has historical importance to the degree that it has exercised a significant influence over the structural change in the homeland, the new home, or both.[2] Here we shall consider the impact of migration only on the countries of Latin America, not on those of origin.

It should be clear also that the original population of the Americas—that is, the ancestors of the Amerindians—will not be considered, since their migration occurred in remote prehistoric times. Nor will we treat the African slaves, because theirs was a transfer far from voluntary. Of course, the introduction of contract laborers bears considerable similarity to the slave trade, but at least there is the presumption that entering into such a contract is a voluntary act; this matter too will be briefly considered.

Above all, however, this study will be concerned with the massive voluntary displacement that in Latin America's case took place between the end of the nineteenth century and the Great Depression. The interregional and intranational migrations that occurred in Latin America during the twentieth century will be outlined only briefly from a historical perspective.

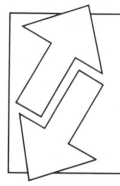

Chapter One

Colonial Antecedents
The Settlement

The Legal Framework:
The Iberian Exclusivist Policy

From its beginnings, emigration from Spain to the New World was strictly regulated by the state.[1] In principle, only Spanish subjects who had proved beyond doubt the "purity" of their blood (that is to say, had proved that they were not descended from Moors or Jews, much less, from gypsies) could emigrate. During the epoch of the Holy Roman Emperor Charles V, who was also king of Castile and Aragón, Catholic subjects of the other kingdoms of the monarch were admitted, but this was a short "liberal" interlude. Yet in spite of the fact that this exclusivist attitude continued to influence colonial legislation, it is clear that many who were not Spanish managed to become established in Spanish America. Either they had become naturalized in Spain before departing, or they had succeeded in deceiving the appropriate authorities.

At first, emigration matters were handled by the House of Trade in Seville. Then, beginning in 1546, the Council of the Indies in Madrid assumed responsibility. Also, many foreigners, after their arrival in Spanish America, were able to obtain an exemption from the existing prohibition at their destination by means of a payment called *composición*. This form of "legal corruption" occurred more and more frequently in the course of the seventeenth century as a reflection of the growing penury of the state, which was dependent upon the income from such sources. The available evidence permits us to deduce that among the immigrants to Spanish America there was always a certain percentage of foreigners and that these tended to settle in the seaports and in the mining centers. Official Spanish exclusivism, manifested from time to time in the expulsion from the Indies of foreigners who were natives of enemy countries, undoubtedly originated for defensive reasons. This exclusivism offers a strong contrast, on the other hand, to the systematic immigration policy practiced by the Crown in the eighteenth century as a means of countering the depopulation of certain provinces of Spain itself.[2]

In the case of Portugal also, by 1600 license was required to emigrate to Brazil, initially populated more often than not by *degredados*, or banished and exiled criminals. Yet in spite of existing prohibitions, immigration to Brazil by diverse non-Portuguese foreigners was tolerated. As in Spanish America, foreigners in Brazil tended to be sailors and merchants. The situation changed around 1700, however, as news of the discovery of gold in Minas Gerais spread and the exodus of people from Portugal and the influx of foreigners into Brazil appeared to reach alarming proportions. Between 1709 and 1720, orders were dispatched prohibiting the entry of foreigners into Brazil and providing for the expulsion of those already present. Moreover, in the face of the depopulation of the northern provinces of Portugal (Minho, Entre-Douro), always the principal source of emigration, a 1720 law prohibited transit to Brazil of all Portuguese subjects who were not traveling on official business. However, once the gold cycle had run its course, controls were relaxed anew and colonization projects sponsored by Crown even came into being. For example, beginning in 1763, attempts were made to encourage the immigration of families from the Azores to Pará, and to found another colony in the extreme south of Brazil.[3]

Approximate Quantitative Framework:
Totals Estimated

The number of Spanish emigrants to the New World can be estimated on the basis of many sources. The most ambitious attempt at investigation so far, by the North American linguist and historian Peter Boyd-

Bowman, has revealed the names of some 55,000 persons who emigrated in the course of the sixteenth century. Boyd-Bowman claims that his sample amounts to roughly 20 percent of the total. By comparing these data with those provided by Pierre Chaunu and Huguette Chaunu on navigation between Spain and the Americas for the years 1504–1650, we can estimate the maximum emigration from sixteenth-century Spain to be some 250,000 persons; and for the half-century that followed,

Table 1. Spanish Migration to the Americas, 1500–1650

	Average tonnage per ship[a]	Average crew per ship[b]	Average passengers per ship[c]	Average total westbound passages[d]
1506–1560	100	30	15	1,781
1541–1560	150	40	20	1,511
Total, 1506–1560				
1561–1600	230	60	30	3,497
Total, 1506–1600				
1601–1625	230	60	30	2,480
1626–1650	300	80	40	1,366
Total, 1601–1650				
Total, 1506–1650				

Sources: Mörner (1976, pp. 766–67); see notes below.

a. Based on Chaunu and Chaunu (1955–58, 6:6:168).

b. Based on Carande (1943, pp. 274–75), who gives minimum crews required for various units of tonnage. See also Chaunu and Chaunu (1955–58, 6:6:305–06) and Parry (1964, p. 85).

c. Our estimate for 1506–60 is somewhat lower than that of Friede (1952, pp. 471–72); however, we maintain his crew / passenger ratio for later periods. Our conjectures in this highly uncertain matter should be conservative.

roughly 200,000, for a total of approximately 450,000 emigrants between 1504 and 1650 (see table 1). On the other hand, we lack even the most rudimentary evidence for estimating, even vaguely, Spanish emigration to America from 1650 to 1810. Nevertheless, it is clear that we are dealing with a sizable emigration from a country that in the 1590s possessed only a population of some eight million.[4]

If we are still far from being able to establish a satisfactory quan-

Average total passengers[e]	Westbound passages in excess of eastbound	Average sailors remaining in the Americas[f]	Estimated total overseas migrants[g]
26,715	689	16,536	43,251
30,220	305	12,200	42,420
			85,671
104,910	1,089	52,272	157,182
			242,853
74,400	769	35,912	111,312
54,640	451	28,864	88,504
			194,816
			436,669

d. Chaunu and Chaunu (1955–58, 6:6:337). Total for 1506–1650 is 10,635 westbound passages.

e. This estimate is based on passengers × voyages; see Chaunu and Chaunu (1955–58, 6:6:337).

f. The deduction should account for mortality during westbound passages and for those returning on other ships. On losses of ships going west, see Chaunu (1955–58, 6:6:861–864).

g. Average number of passengers + average sailors remaining in the Americas.

titative estimate for Spanish emigration to America during the colonial period, the situation is undoubtedly worse in the case of Portuguese emigration to Brazil. The principal authority on Portuguese demographic history, Joel Serrão, assures us that we simply lack the original documentation in series that would serve as a basis for a quantitative calculation (a lack due in part to the destruction caused by the 1755 Lisbon earthquake).[5] Another Portuguese historian has ventured, nonetheless, to estimate the total Portuguese emigration from 1500 to 1580 at 280,000 persons (with an increasing majority destined for Brazil), and at 300,000 between 1580 and 1640. These figures would plunge by one-half between 1640 and 1700. Following the discovery of gold in Brazil, Portuguese emigration increased to about 600,000 during the 1700–60 period, then declined once again. It is necessary to emphasize, of course, that here we are dealing with purely hypothetical conjectures.[6]

European Immigration Prior to 1650

In the first decade after 1492, some 300 Spaniards were sufficient to carry out the Columbus enterprise in the Caribbean. Colonization, in the strict sense of the word, had not even begun before the arrival of 2,500 immigrants in Hispaniola in 1502. During the 1520s and 1530s, the conquest of Mexico and Peru were carried out, as is well known, by small groups of conquistadors, but waves of immigrants would not be long in coming.[7]

Spanish emigration was, by its very nature, spontaneous and voluntary. The state stimulated emigration during certain epochs and for certain categories of people (such as, for example, the friars). On the other hand, as we have noted, it attemped to exclude other categories — Jews and Moorish *conversos* (converted former Moslems), gypsies, and those who had been condemned by the Holy Office of the Inquisition. Subjects of the Kingdom of Aragón were allowed to pass over to the Indies as freely as those of Castile, but other subjects of the monarch were officially excluded, in principle, as were all foreigners, for security reasons. Only between 1526 and 1538, in the non-Spanish domains of Charles V, was a more tolerant policy maintained, a modification that explains the presence of Germans representing the House of

Welser in Venezuela. At all times, however, those who came to the Indies included foreign-born individuals who had been naturalized in Spain in order to obtain passage. Sometimes this involved fraud, or, as already explained, a payment of *composición* to the colonial authorities upon arrival. All in all, we may say that bureaucratic control reduced the migratory influx somewhat. The chronicler López de Velasco notes that "there would have been many more if licenses had been given to all who wished them."[8]

Regulating emigration required a special bureaucratic apparatus attached to the Spanish House of Trade and the Council of the Indies. In turn, this produced an abundance of documents, in the form of reports and licenses for the emigrants, which in large part is preserved in the Archivo General de Indias at Seville. During 1940–46 one such series of licenses appeared in a publication sponsored by the archive. These licenses attest to the departure of 15,480 emigrants in the 1509–59 period. It was claimed when these documents were published that this represented the total emigration for those years. The absurdity of such an assertion was soon demonstrated by the Colombian historian Juan Friede. Pointing to the numerous gaps in the series and to evidence of fraudulent (and thus unrecorded) emigration, Friede suggested that the true total should be at least ten times greater.[9]

Since the mid-1960s, as already noted, a more solid base of information concerning early Spanish emigration has been established concerning some 55,000 identified Spanish emigrants for the sixteenth century. This should constitute between a quarter and a fifth of the total emigration, but Boyd-Bowman's information is insufficient to estimate the real magnitude of this great movement of population. His data do constitute, nonetheless, a satisfactory statistical base from which to calculate percentages. Boyd-Bowman's main purpose in collecting these data was to determine the regional composition of the emigration, viewed, in turn, as the starting point for the development of the diverse Spanish dialects of the New World. His solid, detailed information documents, for example, the predominance of Andalusians, who initially comprised more than one-third of the sample, and later rose to half the total migration.[10]

The traditional image of sixteenth-century emigration is that it was an almost exclusively male phenomenon. One result of the patient compilation of Boyd-Bowman has been to demonstrate how erroneous this generalization is. It is certainly true that in the epoch of the Conquest, from 1520 until 1539, women did not exceed 6 percent of those accounted for in the lists. Nevertheless, toward the middle of the century, the percentage rose to a quarter and even a third of the total (see figure 1). In addition, the emigration of entire families gradually increased as well. Little evidence has appeared, however, concerning the emigrants' ages.[11]

The majority of the emigrants, from the 1520s onward, opted for New Spain (Mexico) as their destination. Nevertheless, during the decades following the discovery of the mountain of silver at Potosí, both Lower and Upper Peru (now Peru and Bolivia), exercised a greater attraction. Between 1540 and 1559, no less than 37 percent of the known emigrants went there. Later, the primacy of New Spain was asserted once again. To judge by the information published by the chronicler Juan López de Velasco, the Spanish population of America should have reached some 150,000 by 1575. His calculation is very tentative, however, based as it is on his data concerning 23,000 *vecinos* (householders) residing in 225 cities and towns inhabited by "Spaniards."[12]

We remain wholly ignorant, in quantitative terms, concerning reemigration. It is true that of the 168 conquistadors in Peru no fewer than 74, perhaps more, returned to Spain. This small, suddenly successful group, however, is extraordinary. Unlike the great majority of immigrants, they were fighters, not settlers. In any case there was from the beginning a reemigrant element, the so-called *indianos* who after years in the New World realized their dream of spending their final years in their homeland. On the other hand, among the disillusioned or failed emigrants in the Indies who had desired to return, probably only a minority were capable of fulfilling their ambition.[13]

It is obvious, then, that Spanish immigration during the sixteenth century was of fundamental importance in the formation of Hispanic American society in every sense. In effect, the early functioning of this society and the success of the colonizing enterprise would have been impossible without a massive and continuous immigratory current.

Moreover, at the present level of our investigation it becomes especially necessary to note the immigration of women from the Iberian peninsula from the earliest times, and especially from around the middle

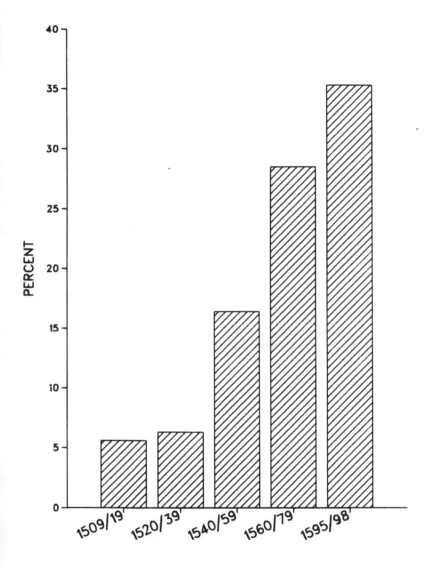

Figure 1. Percentage of Women Among Overseas Spanish Migrants, 1509–1598
Source: Mörner (1982, p. 24), based on Boyd-Bowman (1976b).

of the sixteenth century. What was their role in the augmentation of the population? And what role did they play in the formation of Spanish households in the New World, in comparison with often promiscuous interracial sexual relations?[14] These vital issues remain to be investigated.

Immigration from 1650 Until Independence

Concerning the extent of European immigration during this period, unfortunately, we cannot even obtain an approximate idea, owing to the absence of research. The figure of 52,500 for the eighteenth century, which can be found in a reference work, is merely a conjecture without any real basis. It was derived from registries for merely three selected years at a time when fraudulent migration was abundant.[15] We do know that there were various colonization enterprises during this period. Groups of Basques, Galicians, and others who passed over to Santo Domingo, Texas, Florida, and other frontier territories in this manner between 1700 and 1764, amounted to some 5,000 persons. Montevideo was colonized and populated by other groups. By 1743, forty years after the arrival at Montevideo of the first Canary Islands contingent, there were 100 nuclear families established there, who, when added to soldiers, brought the town's population to 700 persons.[16] The late colonial censuses should be of help in assessing the numbers of Spaniards. But the Chilean census of 1813 is discouraging as a source, since it provides data that are clearly absurd. And the conjectures of the noted scientist Alexander von Humboldt are no more reliable. His estimate that there were 2,500 Spaniards in Mexico City around 1804 is probable, but his assertion that 70,000 *peninsulares* (Spaniards) resided in the entire viceroyalty seems enormously inflated. According to David Brading, the Spaniards of Mexico would total only around 11,000 in 1792. Of these, 5 percent, at the most, were women—a considerable decline in comparison with the late sixteenth century. In a sample of 1,357 men, 48 percent were between the ages of twenty-one and forty, and only 7 percent were youths between eleven and twenty years of age. The remainder were elderly. It would seem that the *gachupines* (Spaniards) of the eighteenth century married in their new country.

There is another sample of considerable interest, though much smaller, from the late eighteenth century. We refer to the wholesale merchants of Buenos Aires between 1778 and 1810, a group carefully researched by Susan Socolow. Out of 142 Buenos Aires merchants (1778–85), no fewer than 112 came from the Iberian Peninsula (79 percent) and another nine from elsewhere in Europe. On the other hand, almost all their wives were born in Buenos Aires or elsewhere in Spanish America (92 percent). More than half of the men were in their thirties when they married, while the great majority of the wives were between fifteen and twenty-four years of age. The "typical" merchant was born in some *pueblo* (small rural town) in the north of Spain and came from the middle or lower-middle strata. He then moved to some larger city before making the voyage to faraway Río de la Plata (two-step migration). Often he would have an uncle there who wanted him to join his business firm. This uncle-nephew relationship in overseas migration can also be observed in other regions and periods of Latin American history. As James Lockhart puts it, with some humor: "The greatest commerce in Spanish America was the importation of nephews on credit, against promises of favor and fortune. [They were] sent for by importunate uncles, pushed out by hard-pressed fathers." Thus the young Spaniard arrived in Buenos Aires at about twenty-four years of age and set out to make a fortune. Socolow finds that the average estate, for a sample of fourteen of her merchants, was no less than 150,000 pesos at the time of their deaths. In social and economic terms, they had made a remarkable career. However, as a consequence of the Spanish laws of inheritance, and because these merchants left six or seven heirs each, such fortunes quickly vanished. Instead, perhaps another nephew or some other young Spanish migrant would repeat the performance.[17]

Regional and Social Composition

Boyd-Bowman's broad sample demonstrates quite clearly the regional composition of Spanish emigration to the New World in the sixteenth century. There was a predominance of Andalusians from the south and Extremadurans from the west, followed by the Castilians from the area around Madrid. It is evident that the emigrants came above all from

Seville in the southwest and from places situated along the principal highways connecting that Andalusian city with the Castilian plateau. Together with other circumstances, this suggests that we are dealing rather with an emigration attracted to the New World (the "pull" forces) than with a movement induced by adverse socioeconomic conditions in the native country ("push" forces).

The data concerning the origins of the Spanish emigrants of the following centuries, suggest that a fundamental structural change must have occurred following Spain's profound social and economic crisis of the seventeenth century. Among emigrants, Basques and Galicians came to dominate, and the percentage of Catalans, Valencians, and Canary Islanders also grew. The north coast and the Canary Islands were considered overpopulated and poor, and the north would also provide the majority of the Spanish emigrants of the nineteenth and twentieth centuries. Taken together, Brading's materials also confirm the impression that radical changes had occurred in the immigrants' regional origins in the seventeenth and eighteenth centuries. Some 64 percent of the late colonial immigrants to Mexico that Brading documents came from the overcrowded north coast of Spain.[18]

Another sample of Spaniards in Mexico City reveals that as early as 1689, the Basques had already reached almost 15 percent of the total.[19] These changes reflected, no doubt, the ever increasing demographic pressure experienced on the north coast, as well as in the Canary Islands, but on the other hand, the economic strength of Catalonia, the provinces around Barcelona, is also reflected, for example, in the departure of many merchants for the New World.

Upon arriving at one of the authorized ports in the colonies, the Spaniards often had to reconsider or, at least, define more specifically their intentions made at the time of departure. Opportunities for earnings related to mining or commerce would no doubt present themselves with greater clarity once in the New World than in Spain. For this reason, the declared destinations of these immigrants at the time of their departure are of little validity. Only in cases of "chain migration," where relatives had sent for other family members, can we be certain of the emigrant's determination to keep to his or her original intention.

It is difficult to generalize concerning the social sources of the Spanish emigrants. Evidently, all social strata were represented—with the exception, so it seems, of the highest—but the proportion of each remains uncertain. On the other hand, the markedly urban character of the emigrants cannot be denied. According to Boyd-Bowman, in the sixteenth century at least 45 percent originated from just thirty-one cities. Of the latter, Seville and Toledo, with less than 2 percent of Spain's population, were responsible for 22 percent of all the emigration overseas. During early times, the role of "marginalized" *hidalgos* or gentry stands out among the hosts of conquistadors, although the artisans and people from rural areas were also notable. Ecclesiastics were numerous. According to one estimate, the religious alone sent to Spanish America throughout the colonial period totaled 15,000. "Servants" were always numerous in the registries, and this could mean a diverse group of persons, ranging from wealthy and educated employees in the service of a colonial administrator down the social scale to the most modest of domestics.[20]

The non-Spanish foreigners who came to settle in Hispanic America in spite of legal obstacles never seem to have constituted more than a small percentage of the total European migrants to the Indies. Originating primarily from Portugal, Italy (especially from Genoa, ever since Columbus), France, and other Mediterranean countries, many of them probably came to the New World as sailors. According to Charles F. Nunn, some 1,500 foreigners are likely to have arrived in Mexico between 1700 and 1760. Toward mid-century, they appear to have comprised about 3 percent of all the European-born of the viceroyalty. Portuguese counted for a third and were followed by Italians, French, and British.[21]

As a result of the Haitian Revolution of 1791, thousands of refugees arrived in the Eastern portion of Cuba where they did much to stimulate the cultivation of coffee. As an example of the suspicious attitude of the Spanish authorities toward all foreigners, we should add that the majority of these "Frenchmen" were soon expelled from Cuba. In 1808, of the 7,500 "French settlers" concentrated in Santiago de Cuba, just 36 percent were whites, while 31 percent were free blacks and mulattoes, and 33 percent slaves.[22]

The Portuguese who emigrated to Brazil seem to have been recruited at first principally from the northern provinces of Portugal (Minho above all), with contingents from Madeira and the Azores coming later.

We should note particularly the presence of farmers and artisans. In addition, as has already been pointed out, Brazil always admitted a marked proportion of non-Portuguese or foreign or immigrants.[23]

Final Observations

Our knowledge of emigration to Latin America during the colonial period is still deficient and very uneven in quality. Nevertheless, we can advance some general observations that will be of interest precisely because they concern the antecedents of the migratory movements of the national period, which is our primary concern.

Despite its limitations, the demographic picture of colonial times indicates a continuous and massive migration. Although much has been said concerning the adventuristic character of Iberian emigration to America, the recent discovery of many letters written to families in Spain by Spanish settlers in the Indies during the sixteenth and seventeenth centuries makes it clear that the hope of improving one's standard of living (such as it was) constituted the most powerful motive in the individual decision.[24] The same may, indeed, be said of the nineteenth-century emigrants, judging by their letters. It is clear, then, that the personal motives behind colonial migration were not substantially different in this respect from those causing the subsequent great migrations. Given the frequent alterations in the populations of the Old World countries, the demographic and social impact of emigration should have been considerable on the countries of origin, at least at the regional level. According to the global estimate of Spanish overseas migration, 1504–1650, already presented (table 1), the annual emigration rate was close to 0.5 per thousand of the total Spanish population around 1590 and 1.4 during the major emigration of around 1580. In accordance with the estimate of a Portuguese historian, the emigration from that country reached 2.5 per thousand in sixteenth-century Portugal, only to rise to 4 per thousand in the eighteenth century.[25] Especially in the case of Portugal, where available data are few, these calculations are highly hypothetical, of course. In the lands of destination, the migratory movement clearly formed the basis for the construction of a society of the European type. Even considering the dynamic of *mestizaje* (racial mixture) from the time of the first migratory generation, the continuous flow of immigrants obviously played a vital role in the formation of a new society. At the same time, it fueled the growth of the powerful tension between peninsular Spaniards and the whites born in America, the Creoles.

In Spain, the respective metropolitan governments strictly regulated the migration, as we have noted, focusing primarily on the adverse political effects of the migratory movement on the mother country. The colonies' need for more and better-qualified immigrants was always secondary in the thoughts and actions of Iberian bureaucrats.

Finally, as we have said, there was always a certain small percentage of immigrants from other countries in both Spanish America and Brazil — a percentage that constituted a direct antecedent of the cosmopolitan migration of the national period. But this group, of uncertain legal status and chiefly made up of persons of humble background, tended to be rapidly assimilated without exercising any apparent important sociocultural influence.[26]

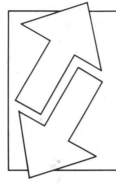

Chapter Two

The Early National Period
New Beginnings

The Emergence of a New Immigration Policy

The Latin American governments established following Independence demonstrated a radically different attitude from that of Spain and Portugal toward non-Iberian immigration. To attract immigrants from countries more powerful than Spain or Portugal seemed a direct route to progress that would save the new countries the effort of educating the "backward" masses of native population. And it also appeared to be the most rapid and efficacious means to remedy the scarcity of labor for plantation agriculture.

In Brazil, by 1810 (that is to say, twelve years before Independence but two years after the arrival of the exiled royal family) authorization had already been granted for naturalized foreigners to become property owners.[1] In the Spanish American countries, the new governments were quick to dictate laws favoring the immigrants, authorizing them to settle and to acquire property. This occurred in the United Provinces of Río de la Plata as early as 1812.[2] On the island of Cuba, too, while it was still a possession of Spain, non-Hispanic immigration was permitted in 1817 with the obvious purpose of counterbalancing the "Africanization" produced by the swelling influx of black slaves demanded by the expanding plantation economy.[3]

In reality, the only requirement imposed by the receiver countries was that the immigrants profess the Roman Catholic religion; and even this condition was suppressed when the liberal parties came to power as occurred in Argentina in 1825. Taking their models of development by and large from the English-speaking world, Latin American liberals considered religious liberty to be essential to an effective immigration policy. For their part, the foreigners of Protestant faith who had already established themselves in the new republics never ceased to insist on religious freedom as a condition of their permanent settlement. In spite of the opposition of the Catholic church, this objective was realized in one country after another. In the case of Mexico, the religious question was for a considerable length of time an insurmountable barrier to the broader kind of immigration desired by the liberals.[4]

When considering the legal aspects of foreign immigration, we should not forget the special situation of the Spanish among the foreigners in Latin America after the colonial period. The traditional hostility between the Iberians and the Creoles worsened during the wars of independence, the result of which was to convert the Spanish-born into "foreigners." In Mexico between 1827 and 1833, three separate expulsions were carried out affecting important contingents of *gachupines*, as the peninsular Spaniards were called. Although Mexico's Spanish community was largely composed of former expeditionary soldiers, of the 2,849 expelled in 1827–28 whose professions are known, curiously the most numerous group (16 percent) were merchants. Again in 1829 merchants were most affected, while regular clergy suffered most in 1833, when the 1829 law regained its force under the liberal government.[5] The hostility was expressed by Spain as well. After abandoning its futile attempts to reconquer its former colonies, Spain for its part took measures to prohibit the emigration of its nationals to the lost territories of Hispanic America by means of legislation enforced between 1836 and 1853. Emigrants from Spain were allowed to go only to Cuba, Puerto Rico, and the Philippines, that is, the colonies that had remained loyal to the mother country.[6]

The Earliest Currents of European Immigrants

The first European immigrants to become established in Latin America following Independence came sometimes as individuals acting on their own and sometimes as members of organized groups participating in an immigration or colonization project.

During this first epoch, until around the middle of the nineteenth century, individual immigration took on a quite heterogeneous character. In the first place, we should mention the peddlers (*mercaderes*), artisans, and sailors who came in growing numbers to the cities and principal ports in search of fortune, following in the footsteps of the small clusters of the same type of immigrants who, despite unfavorable laws, had established themselves during the colonial era. We know the names of some 4,000 persons who entered Brazil individually or with their families between 1810 and 1822, and we know that at least one-quarter of them were merchants. Of this number, more than 1,500 were Spanish, approximately 1,000 were French, 600 were English, 200 were German, and 200 were Italian. Portuguese were not included in the total.[7]

Second, we should take note of a new category, military immigrants. In the armies of Bolívar, there were some 7,000 British and Irish volunteers who played a decisive role in the anti-Spanish struggle in South America. Of the 1,000 survivors of these volunteers a great many opted to remain, and the same could be said of the German veterans of the army launched by Brazil's Emperor Pedro I against Argentina in 1826–27.[8] Other military men, generally officers, had come without clearly defined plans; many were bored in postwar Europe, and came to Latin America simply in search of adventure. For example, many officers came from Sweden, an especially tranquil country.[9]

Gradually other diverse elements began to arrive, of both aristocratic and bourgeois origin, for whom the search for adventure in an exotic New World was intermixed with politico-ideological motives that had led them to leave their homes. We refer, for example, to the exiled Italian revolutionaries who began to arrive in 1820, among whom none was more notable than Giuseppe Garibaldi (who would become, later on, a great hero in his own country), and to the military men and intellectuals who had participated, in some cases as leaders, in the revolutions of 1848 in Hungary and other countries. In the majority of these cases, however, a sojourn in Latin America does not appear to have been a true immigration but rather a mere episode in a life of uprootings and exile.[10]

There was no lack of those who settled in Latin America by mere chance. In 1850, for example, 106 Norwegians headed for California in search of gold were stranded in Rio de Janeiro when their ship was unable to continue its voyage. The majority of these passengers remained in South America and participated in the founding of Colonia Dona Francisca in Santa Catarina.[11]

In a number of cities, especially seaports, there developed prosperous and self-conscious foreign communities led by great merchants. Notwithstanding national rivalries within these communities, they usually presented a remarkably united front whenever facing abuse or hostility on the part of authorities or rioting crowds native to the host country. The travelogues written by European visitors can tell us a great deal about the mentality and nature of these foreign enclaves. For example, a German visiting the Chilean mining district of Copiapó in 1859 tells us how, faced by the threat of revolutionary violence, all the foreigners joined in forming special militia units to protect themselves and their property. Our German was the chief of one of them. His picturesque account illustrates how the solidarity and self-defense of the foreigner could easily lead to actual intervention in local affairs, however justified or not it appeared to be. In other cases, foreign property was indeed destroyed and confiscated. Then intervention could instead take the shape of the dispatch of the foreign man-of-war, that is, the infamous "gunboat diplomacy."[12]

An especially dense concentration of immigrants developed in Uruguay, a country that received, between 1835 and 1842, around 33,000 foreign settlers; the largest single contingent were the French, principally from the Pyrenees region, some of whom spoke the Basque language. Many of these had first settled in Argentina, but were driven out during the troubled years 1842–51, when the region was beset by civil war. Together with Argentine liberals, they had crossed the river from Buenos Aires in search of refuge during the Rosas dictatorship. They were originally attracted to the Río de la Plata region by the liberal colonization policy launched by Argentine President Bernardino Rivadavia during the mid-1820s. Others came directly to Montevideo, attracted by the favorable business climate that existed there until the city came under a lengthy siege from 1842 to 1851 (a part of the so-called *Guerra Grande*). In 1843, no less than 60 percent of Montevideo's 31,000 inhabitants were foreigners.[13]

Colonization projects, which were normally aimed at the countryside, generally had their origin in the profit motives of some individual, or a European entrepreneurial group. Given the demand for immigrants, and the expectations and the inexperience of the Latin American governments in dealing with such entrepreneurs, recruitment and colonization projects were readily approved by the authorities in the host country. To mention Uruguay once again, a native entrepreneur was responsible for bringing some 850 Canarians there in the 1830s and 1840s. About 40 percent of this contingent were women; as many as a third of the total were children under fifteen. Another very spectacular project of this type was carried out in 1819 when 2,000 Swiss, the majority of them complete families, settled in Brazil and founded the town of Nova Friburgo in the highlands of the Province of Rio de Janeiro. Two years of shortages, unemployment, and even hunger, had created in Switzerland an atmosphere propitious for emigration, which explains the large number of participants and the favorable attitude of the Swiss authorities toward the project. This migratory enterprise took a great toll in human life: almost 19 percent died in crossing—primarily, it would seem, as a result of malaria contracted during an unnecessarily prolonged stay in a marshy district of Holland. Moreover, the site selected in Brazil proved to be inappropriate for a colony; mortality in the town from the outset was very high; and, finally, the Brazilian authorities lost interest in the project. As a consequence of all these factors, Nova Friburgo continued to be a failure. We know this from the testimony of some of its settlers who abandoned the colony in order to seek elsewhere the prosperity they had longed for.[14]

Another ambitious immigration project for European colonization concerned Baja Verapaz, to the northeast of the capital of Guatemala, in 1834–44. The plan was initiated by the liberal president, Mariano Gálvez, but its realization remained in the hands of a group of entrepreneurs—at first British, later Belgian—who were for the most part inept speculators who knew nothing about transporting immigrants and establishing colonies. As in the case of Nova Friburgo, the Verapaz experiment demonstrated the formidable obstacles to the introduction of agriculture of the European type in a subtropical setting.[15]

Obviously, colonization projects in temperate climates where the weather and terrain were more familiar to Europeans held out greater possibilities for success, or at least for survival. Thus, the German colonies in the extreme south of Brazil were not long in achieving a relative prosperity, in spite of their disastrous beginnings. José Bonifacio de Andrada e Silva, a noted statesman, had dreamed of an "agricultural-military" frontier colonization of the Cossack type in Brazil. Charged with the responsibility for the project was a notorious adventurer, George Anton von Schäffer, who created an unscrupulous recruitment company in Germany. Between 1824 and 1830, some 5,350 Germans arrived in Rio Grande do Sul. São Leopoldo, founded in 1824, became the first of numerous German colonies in the region formed by small independent agricultural proprietors. In São Leopoldo family plots were established consisting initially of twenty-four hectares.[16]

With the fall of Brazil's Emperor Pedro I in 1831, German immigration to Río Grande do Sul was interrupted. It was not renewed until 1850, when new contingents arriving from Germany formed additional centers of colonization in this and other provinces of the Brazilian South. Dr. Herman N. Blumenau, an honest and singularly efficacious person, gave his name to the most successful colony, which was founded in 1850 in the province of Santa Catarina. Another successful settlement founded in the same region was Dona Francisca which bore the name of a sister of Pedro II, the wife of the Prince of Joinville. It seems to have had a larger middle-class component than the other colonies, possibly liberals disenchanted with the consequences of the European revolutions of 1848.[17]

During the same period, other Germans initiated, in the forests of Valdivia and Llanquihue of southern Chile, a colonization project that in time achieved considerable well-being. Three thousand pioneers were established there between 1846 and 1858.[18] In Argentina, the political situation continued to be much less stable than in Chile and Brazil during this era. Nevertheless, in Argentina too various attempts were made to establish agricultural colonies, especially with Swiss and French settlers. An early and disastrous project of 1824 consisted in inviting the "unemployed poor of Great Britain and Ireland" to establish themselves in the region of Entre Rios.[19]

Quite different from all the land colonization schemes were the occasional attempts to encourage labor immigration for European enterprises in other sectors. In 1824, for example, a British mining company established itself in Pachuca—Real del Monte—in Mexico. Within a few years it had brought no less than 330 miners from Cornwall to work in the mines. Even after a new company took over in mid-century, the special relation between these mines and Cornish mining know-how continued. Smaller groups of specialists were active there until 1906.[20]

It is impossible to measure with any precision the size of these first migratory currents directed toward Latin America. But it has been suggested that between 1816 and 1850 some 200,000 Europeans entered Brazil, Argentina, and Uruguay, the countries which were no doubt the most attractive.[21]

In spite of numerous discouraging experiences, the Latin American elites of this period never lost their positive attitude toward European immigration, an attitude that reflected in part their obvious scorn for the masses of their own countries as well as a lack of faith in the possibility of forming a native class of responsible small farmers (*labradores*) by means of popular education and the improvement of the conditions of life in the countryside. Nor did the advocates of white immigration cease to possess influence in spite of the political risk involved in massive foreign colonization of border zones—a risk eloquently demonstrated by the seccession of Mexico's Texas colonies in 1835. Although during the first half of the nineteenth century immigration to Latin America was sporadic, involved relatively small numbers of people, and had generally ephemeral results, it later became in some countries a mass phenomenon. For the process to achieve its full potential, all that was lacking were circumstances strengthening "push factors" in the countries of origin plus a reduction in the costs of the journey; and in the countries of destination, greater political stability and the abolition of slavery—this crucial final requirement being necessary to upgrade the conditions of free labor. In the Brazilian province of Santa Catarina, slavery had been prohibited in 1848 and was abolished in the Province of Río Grande do Sul a few years later, although in the empire as a whole it lingered on until 1888.[22]

The Substitution of Contract Workers for Slaves

During the first half of the nineteenth century, the African slave trade encountered increasing difficulties. The two principal markets for this human "merchandise," Brazil and Cuba, ceased the importation of slaves by 1855 and 1865, respectively. But much earlier it could be foreseen that, owing to the brief life expectancy of the slaves in the Latin American plantation areas and their low rate of reproduction, slavery as an institution was doomed in the long run. To take a single example, in British Guiana between 1820 and 1832, the life expectancy of a slave hardly reached twenty-three years. Even after abolition, the net rate of natural population increase continued to be low. Nevertheless, thanks to contract immigration, the population of Guiana would be almost three times as high in 1891 as in 1844.[23]

The owners of plantations, who complained of the "scarcity of labor" (motivated actually by their resistance to providing adequate pay and treatment for workers), were inclined in these circumstances toward another solution of the labor problem: the immigration of theoretically free contract laborers. In order to pay back the price of their long voyage, poor immigrants were required to commit themselves to work for their patrons in the new country for more or less lengthy periods and with fixed minimal salaries. This mode of solving the planters' problem would provide mainly "coolie" labor, that is to say, poor Asian workers, mostly Chinese males. But others also succumbed to this false temptation to escape the misery of their homelands, including some groups of white proletarians, principally from Madeira, the Azores, and the Canary Islands.[24] In the 1830s, there was still the hope of attracting whites who might later "supply a middle class . . . and set an example of industry to the Negroes," as planter attitudes would have it. These pious expectations of the planters were, in general, not realized, but in Guiana more than a few Madeirans managed to survive. Contract labor typically resulted in premature death in servitude before the required period of service was completed and longed-for freedom was achieved.[25]

China was the principal provider of workers who migrated to the Spanish-speaking countries by means of this system. A total of 142,000 contract laborers arrived from Shanghai and Canton at Cuban ports between 1847 and 1874—that is to say, while slavery still existed in the island but when it was also becoming more evident that African slaves were insufficient to satisfy the demand for cheap labor in the expanding sugar industry. Mortality was very high among the Chinese. Even before arriving in Cuba, some 16,000 (or just over 10 percent) died during the long and arduous voyage from China. In 1874, only 68,000 Chinese remained in Cuba, where mortality was also heavy, and very few were ever able to reemigrate. But human suffering was of little concern to the employers. A merchant dryly commented in 1860: "Supposing that 600 men were shipped from China, and that only 300 arrived in Cuba, these would cover all the losses and still leave a brilliant profit."[26]

Some 75,000 Chinese entered Peru between 1849 and 1874—that is to say, contemporaneously with abolition (1854). They labored in the coastal plantations, carried out the highly undesirable and often fatal task of extracting guano, and built railroads. Meiggs and Keith, the notorious pair of dynamic North American entrepreneurs who employed Chinese in Peru, later implemented the same system in Costa Rica. As with the Chinese bound for Cuba, mortality 1847–59, was very high. Whereas 87,000 Chinese left for Peru, perhaps 15 percent perished during the crossing, a death rate higher than that of the earlier Chinese migration to Cuba, although the latter involved a much longer voyage. On the Atlantic slave route, the mortality rate among the enslaved Africans had by the eighteenth century already become several percentage points lower.[27]

In other respects, too, the transport of Chinese contract laborers closely resembled the slave trade. Rebellions among the passengers were frequent, in response to notoriously bad treatment. In the countries of destination the Chinese suffered yet more harsh treatment, which also was reflected in their high mortality. They lived in isolation, imprisoned and without access to women; their patrons accused them of homosexual practices and on this pretext abused them all the more. Those workers who survived for the stipulated labor period, although suffering indignities perhaps as great as those endured by the African slaves, might eventually move up the social scale, especially within the urban middle class.[28] But for many, at least in Cuba, only a second fraudulent "contract" awaited them and, if they refused this, unpaid service to the state under much the same conditions as the *libertos*—African bondsmen deposited on the Cuban coasts by the British navy.

In the British Caribbean possessions and Guiana, four of every five contract laborers came, not surprisingly, from India, the principal dominion of the British Empire. There were also workers from Africa, China, and Madeira, totaling over half a million individuals arriving in these lands between the abolition of slavery in 1833 and 1918. It is worth noting that no less than 8,000 African "volunteers" followed the route of the slaves to settle in Jamaica between 1840 and 1865. In Dutch Guiana, now Suriname, after the abolition of slavery in 1863, first Chinese were brought in; then, between 1873 and 1917, 34,000 contract laborers arrived from Indonesia and India. Another 25,000 Indonesians and Indians entered Martinique between 1853 and 1884.[29]

The contracts stipulated that workers could return to their countries of origin without cost after having served for the specified number of years. But the reality of the work situation proved to be quite unrelated to such contract terms. Only a minority were able to take advantage of this clause, or did so, anyway. In the case of workers from India, 32 percent reemigrated from British Guiana, and 34 percent from Dutch Guiana.[30] As a result, all of these labor migrations contracted for the Caribbean, the Guianas and the coast of Peru left their indelible mark on the ethnic map of these countries.

In other plantation societies, contract labor never was an important factor. Brazil, for example, was able to attract only between 2,000 and 3,000 Chinese. During the Brazilian empire, a scarcity of labor manifested itself rather late. When around 1880 requests were finally made directly to the Chinese imperial government to obtain contract laborers, the Chinese authorities already possessed eloquent testimony of the enslavement to which so many Chinese had been reduced in the Americas, and they simply refused to cooperate.[31]

The exploitation of the abused Asians seems frequently to have been marked by racial prejudice, but, as we have said, the treatment of contracted whites was apparently not much better. The poor Canary Islanders destined for Cuba during the 1850s, for example, had to accept explicitly that their wages would be much lower than those of "the free laborers and slaves of the island." They were also forced to accept work schedules of at least twelve hours a day, although, of course these were considerably shorter hours than those of slaves on the sugar plantation during the harvest.[32]

In São Paulo, Brazil, the cultivation of coffee enjoyed its first expansion around the middle of the nineteenth century. The work was carried out by African slaves, but the slave trade was still threatened with extinction because of the persecution initiated by Great Britain many years earlier. In 1847, a great São Paulo coffee *fazendeiro* (plantation owner), Nicolau Vergueiro, initiated an experiment using European contract laborers. But the Swiss and German immigrants demanded better treatment than the planters were willing to concede to them, accustomed as the planters were to the forced servitude of slaves. In 1856 a riot broke out on the Ibicaba *fazenda* (plantation). Soon after, the Paulista coffe growers returned to their previous complete dependence upon slave labor, obtainable now by inter-regional trade in human chattel from the less prosperous areas to the Northeast.[33]

We may observe, then, that the essential factor in the denigration and unrelenting exploitation of the contract laborers was not their color, but rather their isolation, imposed by the great distance from their native countries. In these conditions employers could easily force upon them an iron work discipline without awakening the solidarity of other exploited strata in the society, and compel them to accept minimal remuneration, which at the same time served to maintain the low level of agricultural wages for free laborers. But we should not lose sight of the fact that contract labor was, for those who survived, a servitude that finally came to an end. As we have already pointed out, for more than a few of the Chinese workers, it was the starting point of their eventual entry into the urban middle class. In the British Caribbean, especially in Trinidad and Guiana, at least two-thirds of the immigrants who came from India would not return to their homes as they had originally intended: they too opted to remain and came to form, in time, a free and modestly successful, enterprising peasantry.

Three Case Studies: Argentina, Uruguay, and the Spanish Colony of Cuba[34]

Argentina

It became the policy of President Bernardino Rivadavia to subdivide the pampa according to a system of emphyteusis, applied during 1824–26, by granting twenty-year leases to individuals who would pay an annual rent equal to 8 percent of production on pasture and 4 percent on farm land. This would have been a splendid policy in terms of stimulating immigration, had it been maintained. However, the new landholders frequently reneged on their annual payments, and, in order to derive badly needed government income, the dictator Juan Manuel de Rosas forgave these debts and regularized ownership—a concept not contemplated in emphyteusis—in exchange for cash settlements, to be considered as purchase price.

Immigration to the pampa began in earnest in the 1840s with German arrivals, but emigration from Germany was soon shut off by Prussia, in response to ill-treatment of earlier settlers. Entry by Europeans renewed in the 1850s, following a trend toward parcelization. Buenos Aires Province provides an example, as historian Jonathan Brown has demonstrated.[35] A country containing roughly a half million people in 1810 grew to 1,800,000 as the first census was concluded in 1869. By this time, at least 75 percent of the Argentine population lived in rural areas, and mass immigration had begun on a large scale.[36]

Uruguay

Early immigration is better known in Uruguay, thanks in part to the work of Juan Antonio Oddone.[37] With the guarantee of Uruguayan independence by Great Britain after 1827, a group of 700 immigrants arrived at Montevideo in 1833 from the Canary Islands. An agreement was signed with Spain in 1835 to promote immigration, but under the dictatorship of Rosas the government at Buenos Aires established a naval blockade at the port of Montevideo, one result of which was to restrict the flow until the dictator's fall in 1851. Between 1835 and 1842 roughly 33,000 Europeans did arrive; at least 6,400 of these were from France, while 2,500 came from England. Rosas's siege of Montevideo from 1842 until 1851 not only cut off arrivals but actually encouraged the flight of small capitalists and the departure of foreigners. Some 8,000 French passed over to Buenos Aires and Montevideo's population declined by roughly 25 percent. In 1843 the population of the Uruguayan capital had been at least two-thirds foreign-born, of whom some 4,000 were Italians. As a result of the French exodus, Italians gained numerical superiority, though the French retained the lead in landownership. A return emigration from Buenos Aires to Montevideo followed the fall of Rosas and the reopening of the Uruguayan port in 1851.

By 1852 more than a fifth of the Uruguayan population was foreign-born. In 1853 the first "Sociedad Protectora de Inmigrantes" was founded. Work was plentiful in the cattle industry and the *saladeros* (salted beef plants), due to expansion of the British market for Uruguayan meat. The 1860 census revealed that the proportion of foreigners in Uruguay had grown to 35 percent. Brazilians now constituted the largest foreign colony, almost 20,000 people, or a fourth of the foreign total. Spaniards ran a close second with some 18,000. The Italian and French colonies had stabilized at 10,000 and 9,000, respectively. Almost half the population of Montevideo itself was now foreign-born.[38]

Cuba

Cuba presents a case under continuing Spanish colonialism in the nineteenth century, as well as another instance of inhibition of immigration dictated by the continuing expansion of slavery. Colonial authorities and planters alike had desired white immigration to counteract the impact of black slaves on the population's racial balance, at least since the Haitian Revolt of 1791. The colonial government established a "Junta of Agriculture" in 1791 and invited Canary Islanders to enter Cuba. Between the junta's creation and 1847, the regime would bring in Mexican Indians and Chinese as well, in an effort to slow African importation. The greatest success was in attracting refugees from Haiti–Santo Domingo. The French were granted free entry until 1807, when Charles IV of Spain reversed the policy and began expelling the French from Cuba. Anti-French riots occurred in Havana in 1809, but Ferdinand VII reopened Cuba to non-Spanish immigration by 1817, after Napoleon's fall. As a result of the law of 1817, some 1,183 foreigners in Cuba obtained the *carta de domicilio* (residency card) between 1818 and 1820. Of these, 436 were French, 158 were from the United States, and 76 were German. The most numerous professional groups were farmers (360) and carpenters (308).[39]

All who came were required to be Roman Catholic, of course, and each family member was promised eight acres of land, plus four acres per slave imported, and a fifteen-year exemption from taxation. To carry out the program, a Junta of White Population was created at Havana, whose goal was to encourage immigration by Spanish citizens, especially islanders.

With this effort under way, Spain signed a treaty with England in 1817 ostensibly "abolishing" the slave trade. Henceforth, a tax of six pesos per imported male slave was required by the junta to discourage slave importation and to support "propagation of the [white] race." By 1821 the junta had received over 300,000 pesos and could offer handsome financial arrangements to white immigrants: transportation, lodging, hospital care, and cash maintenance for newly arrived adults and children for up to three months.

Individuals with property carried out the program, subdividing their land tracts and selling to each adult immigrant between 1,500 to and 3,000 acres. The recipient paid 100 pesos after two years, to be followed by four yearly payments of 25 pesos each, and ten yearly payments of 50 pesos each. These landlord-contractors received 60 pesos per adult European and half as much per non-European brought. In addition, as "founders of towns," entreprenuers received numerous advantages, including civil and criminal jurisdiction in these lands for life.

Restoration in Cuba of the Liberal Spanish Constitution, 1820–23, suspended the program. The junta in Cuba regained authority in 1823, however, and efforts continued, though achieving only minimal success until 1834. By that date, immigrants began to arrive on their own; 35,000 Europeans had come by 1843, a figure that exceeded slave imports.

Spanish policy changed in 1835 in favor of white immigration to Cuba—the result of British efforts to enforce a recently signed second treaty suppressing the slave trade. A new Junta of Development was formed in Cuba with a new purpose: to bring laborers, not colonists. Both abolitionists and planters in search of free European labor joined in the new effort. The desire to end dependence on slavery gave rise to the notion of an "ideal sugar mill," operated by Europeans and supplied by small cane farmers. Spanish peasants were brought during the 1840s, but landlords insisted on treating them as tenants. When the pro-immigration interests came to be indentified with the cause of independence, the Spanish hastily decided to withdraw their support for the experiment, and by 1843 the effort had ended, having stimulated an unseemly speculation in land. The great planters had turned against the plan as well, since it clashed with their desires for future access to large unfettered tracts of land, for sugar expansion.

Despite the British blockade, after 1843 Spain authorized Cubans to turn anew to Africa for slaves, but by 1847 the planters were looking to Mexico for Mayans and to Portuguese traders for Chinese. The availability of Mayans resulted from the desperate financial straits of the state government of Yucatan confronting an expensive rebellion of the Huits, or unacculturated frontier Mayan Indians, who desired to drive the Mexicans from the peninsula. Necessity and opportunism dictated that few of those sold to Cuba were actually Huits, however, since the peaceful Mayans were more easily captured by the *dzulob*, or white minority.[40]

In the 1850s immigration by both the Chinese and the Spanish resumed. Companies were established to import Galicians, and thousands arrived. But the companies failed and the Chinese source was proffered once again. Between 1852 and 1874 some 125,000 were brought in on spurious contracts, a trade in human labor that was slowed only by Cuba's Ten Years' War for Independence (1868–78).

It was only after the war, which the Spanish won at great cost to Cuba, that a new and more successful emphasis would be given to white immigration, and this would occur simultaneously with the gradual abolition of slavery (1880–86). Cuba would then become a stepping-stone for emigrants from Spain en route to other parts of the former Spanish colonies.[41]

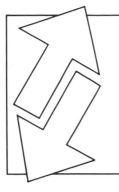

Chapter Three

Mass Immigration
The European Context and
the Selection of Latin America

The European Context

During the nineteenth century, mainly because
of a rapid decline in the mortality rate, the European population began
to increase, growing from a rate of 5.8 per thousand in 1841–50 to 9.9
in 1891–1900. This began in the northwest of Europe (where the rate of
population increase in Great Britain and Ireland was 13.7 per thousand
in 1821–30), and gradually spread to the countries of southern and
eastern Europe. European population grew from 187 million in 1800, to
266 million in 1850, to 401 million in 1900 — more than doubling in one
century. This created a demand for food that could not be satisfied by
traditional agriculture, and agricultural modernization was slow and
incomplete, especially in southern and eastern Europe.

Two profoundly important parallel processes, industrialization and
urban development, spread in a similar way, first, to Great Britain and
then to other parts of Europe. However, these two phenomena were
insufficient, or were too slow, to absorb the human surplus produced by
the demographic explosion. This is the principal reason why more than
50 million Europeans emigrated overseas for four generations between
1830 and 1930.[1] (See map 1.)

The first migratory waves, consisting primarily of North Europeans,
were bound primarily for the United States, which offered a culture and
environment similar to that of the European homeland and clear opportunities for advancement. Latin America became important much later,

35

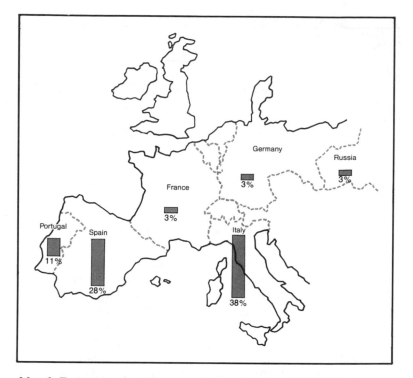

Map 1. Emigration from Europe to Latin America, 1854–1924
Source: Mörner (1982b, p. 31).

when southern and eastern Europe began to experience accelerated population growth such as occurred, for example, in the former Polish territories which had been divided among Russia, Prussia, and Austria. This population increase coincided with a crucial economic phenomenon. Beginning in 1870, great quantities of cheap cereals, cultivated principally by the European immigrants in the midwestern United States, began to reach European markets, alleviating the food shortage but provoking at the same time a genuine agricultural crisis in southern and eastern Europe. The natural consequences was that more immigrants from these countries joined the migratory waves of the years 1870–1910.[2]

During the same period, the price of passage was considerably reduced owing to the replacement of sailing craft by great steamships.

By 1888, three-quarters of the oceangoing vessels arriving in Argentine ports were powered by steam. Partly as a result, British tonnage registered in these ports tripled over a twelve-year period. It is likely that by the 1870s steamships were transporting more immigrants than were sailing ships. Julio Lorenzoni, a young Italian who crossed the Atlantic by steamship with his family in 1877, reports that the price of the passage from Genoa to Rio de Janeiro fluctuated between 100 and 150 lire in those days. In just three years, from 1903 until 1906, prices fell from 165 to 80 lire for the Italy to the Río de la Plata run. Moreover, the voyages had come to be much less risky. During the 1903–25 period, the mortality rate on voyages between Italy and South America was only four persons per thousand.[3] In addition, as we shall see, passages were frequently subsidized by the authorities or by patrons in the countries of destination. As a result, the transatlantic migratory movement of this second phase included members of the poorest strata of the countries of origin, which was hardly the case during the first period.

Let us also briefly note some specific factors influencing the migratory rates from the countries that were most important for Latin America. In Italy, the coincidence of a downturn in the economy and competition from cheap grain imports from overseas provoked an especially severe crisis between 1885 and 1895. In these circumstances, emigration from the northern Italian provinces dominated, notwithstanding their greater economic development and better living conditions relative to the South. In southern Italy, the structural problems of an extremely impoverished and backward society continued to worsen, as a result of population increase, until the turn of the century. By that time, the situation in the North had improved; consequently, contingents of Italians from the South predominated during the more recent period.[4] One should not exaggerate the correlation between the level of misery and that of emigration, however. A southern region like Apulia could be very poor, and yet might have a relatively low level of migration. But, upon closer examination, we discover that the level of socialist militancy was very high in Apulia; this, it seems, was an alternative to emigration.

In Spain, the removal of legal obstacles to emigration in 1853 was obviously a stimulus to mass emigration. The exodus came at first from two overpopulated areas, Galicia and the Canary Islands. In Galicia, *caciquismo*, or boss rule, usury, and a peculiar type of small-scale tenancies (*foros*) were the deep-rooted evils that spurred emigration. The rate of emigration from the Canary Islands was influenced by the crisis in the staple crop, cochineal, as a result of the introduction of synthetic anilines beginning in 1870. But the emigratory movement was also important in other peripheral Spanish regions, such as Catalonia, which had a vigorously expanding economy and higher standard of living; in this case, we must assume the influence of "pull" factors. On the other hand, the interior of Spain was little affected. Quantitatively, Spanish emigration reached its peak in 1912–13.[5]

In Portugal, as in other periods of Portuguese history, it was the northern provinces with their minifundia and high population density that fed the migratory stream crossing the Atlantic. In the early 1890s, the vineyards of that area were destroyed by plant lice, the dreaded phylloxera. Demand for labor declined, and emigration reached its culmination in 1895. There followed another peak in 1912.[6]

In Eastern Europe, the beginning of transatlantic emigration is clearly related to the agrarian crisis of the 1880s. The Polish territories incorporated into the Russian Empire experienced veritable "emigration fevers" that led numbers of exploited peasants to seek their fortunes in Brazil in 1890–91 and again in 1911–12. In the case of Galicia, an impoverished area of Poland under Austrian domination, there were similar migratory waves between 1895 and 1914. Emigration from the Polish territories under Prussian rule began much earlier, declining about 1890. In the future it would be primarily directed toward the United States. The Jews who lived in various regions of the vast Russian Empire were driven to emigrate by the persecution to which they were subjected, especially the bloody pogroms of 1881–84 and 1903–07. It should also be noted that some East European governments encouraged minority emigration to ease such problems.

The countries that provided the bulk of the emigrants to Latin America between 1880 and the First World War—Italy, Spain, Portugal, and Russia—had been poor for many years. Not only was agriculture at a primitive level in these countries, but also they were the least industrialized parts of Europe during this period and their rate of economic growth remained quite sluggish.[7] Workers' wages in Spain, Portugal, Italy, and Russia were the lowest in Europe in 1865; only Italian wages, which could buy twice as much wheat in 1896 as in 1871, improved during the latter part of the century.

The Choice of Latin America

We have already noted the "push" factors responsible for the mass emigration of Europeans during the second half of the nineteenth century and the early years of the twentieth (see map 2). The majority of those emigrants opted for a new life in the United States, attracted by its expanding frontiers and strong economy, its liberal policy facilitating the acquisition of land (the Homestead Act of 1862), and the relative stability of its institutions, particularly following the Civil War of 1861–65. In addition, the voyage from the European Atlantic coast to New York was shorter and cheaper than the voyage to Buenos Aires or Sydney, and the climatic and geographical conditions in North America were generally more familiar to Europeans. Even the Latin American countries with the most favorable political and geographical conditions were in no position to compete seriously in all these aspects.

It is appropriate to ask, then, why some eleven million Europeans— that is to say, one-fifth of the total transatlantic emigration—nevertheless chose a Latin American destination. We observe, for example, that 68 percent of the Italian transatlantic emigrants between 1875 and 1898 embarked for Latin America, and the same was true of more than 70 percent of Portuguese emigrants between 1855 and 1921, as well as for the great majority of the Spanish emigrants, following the reduction of Spanish emigration to North Africa in the 1880s.[8]

It is obvious that in the selection of a country of destination, cultural affinity and a common or similar language play a considerable role.[9] Yet nineteenth-century Spanish emigration promoted few cultural links between Spain and its former colonies. Moreover, as many as one-fourth of the total immigrants to Brazil and one-seventh of those to Argentina at the time came from non-Latin countries.[10] We must therefore conclude that other factors were also involved.

We should consider economic factors, first of all, given that the principal motive for this mass transfer was clearly the immigrants' desire to better their material situation. The principal mechanism draw-

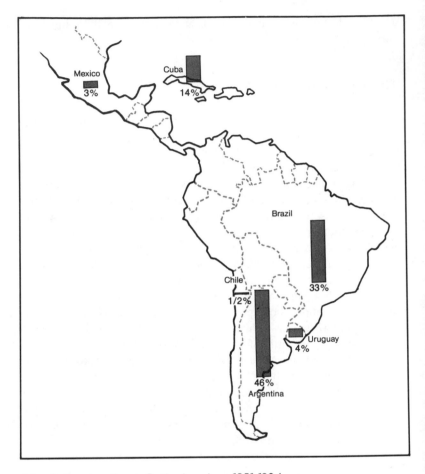

Map 2. Immigration to Latin America, 1851-1924
Source: Mörner (1982b, p. 31).

ing immigrants to Latin America was the expansion of the European market for Latin American products. To satisfy this growing demand, a larger and "better" work force was needed, which in turn induced various Latin American countries to carry out an active immigration policy.

Viewed more closely, immigratory evolution may be seen to have followed somewhat distinct paths in each country. Each felt the impact of favorable or adverse conditions, so that one cannot generalize too far about the basic operating forces affecting Latin American immigration at all times.

In Argentina—a sparsely populated country, dominated by a ranching oligarchy linked to the exportation of hides, and an importer of wheat until the 1870s—a handful of European colonists, induced with great difficulty to settle in the Province of Santa Fe, became pioneers in growing wheat. With impressive rapidity, the settlers advanced from cultivation for the local market to massive exportation of wheat for the international market.[11] It was only then, toward the end of the 1880s, that the oligarchy began to favor mass immigration (which had hardly been necessary for a less labor-intensive pastoral economy), although this goal had been proclaimed at least thirty years earlier by liberal leaders like Juan Bautista Alberdi (famous for his assertion, "To govern is to populate"), and Domingo Faustino Sarmiento. Initially, immigrants to Argentina had to pay for their voyages, although the government arranged for low fares from the shipping lines. In 1888, however, the government began to subsidize passages. The crisis of 1890 soon forced Argentina to suspend the practice due to the finanical squeeze, but during these two years, it had subsidized one-third of the immigration (125,000 individuals).[12] Fares continued to be low, however. It should be noted that around 1900, an agricultural laborer could be reimbursed for the cost of the voyage to Argentina with just two weeks' work.

In Uruguay, the authorities never took such active measures. But the comparatively high level of workers' wages near the end of the 1880s, just when European emigration was on the rise constituted a most effective stimulus to immigration.[13] The same occurred in Argentina around 1900. It is estimated that in 1904 the cost of food absorbed just 25 percent of a worker's wages in Argentina, compared to 28 percent in Australia, 33 percent in the United States, and 60 percent in Italy and Spain.[14]

In Brazil, a shortage of laborers in the coffee industry of São Paulo became critical in 1888, when slavery was abolished. This led to a policy of subsidized immigration on a grand scale, financed in part after 1891 by the state of São Paulo. Between 1889 and 1893, the number of immigrants entering the state with subsidized passages fluctuated between 82 and 99 percent. It remained high until 1902 when the Italian government, reacting against abuses committed against immigrants, prohibited emigration on subsidized fares. The free passages from Genoa to Santos explain why so many poor Italian immigrants chose to sail for Brazil, a country about which they probably knew little or nothing.[15]

Both the Latin American governments interested in obtaining immigrants and the shipping companies in search of passengers found natural allies in the emigration agencies. Many agencies, prompted by an unscrupulous profit motive, attempted by any means to assure that the potential emigrant selected whatever country they represented. Their pamphlets contained a mixture of truth and falsehood, and they used agents of all types. In 1870, we find a priest in the Venetian countryside acting as an agent—a combination of occupations that probably inspired undue confidence. Frequently the agents' activities exceeded legal limits. For example, they clandestinely assisted the emigration of those who desired to evade military service. Other agents were genuine "buyers of children," and they were sometimes involved in white slavery. In the Russian Empire, such activities were prohibited, but in 1913 some 170 illegal agents were uncovered there. In the 1890s, an agent with headquarters in Udine, northwest of Venice, managed to spread propaganda causing a genuine "Brazilian fever" among the peasants of faraway Western Galicia—an extremely poor and exploited group. The reason: a contract signed in 1892 between Brazil and a large shipping company aimed at attracting a great many immigrants. Another wave of peasants from this region was recruited by the agents of construction and railroad companies, including the "Madeira-Mamoré" railroad enterprise, of sad memory. Thousands of immigrants contracted to construct this railroad in the midst of the jungle; once there, they succumbed to very real fevers. It is evident, then, that the shipping agents were largely responsible for the selection of Latin American countries as destinations for European emigrants. Otherwise, we could not explain, for example, why some 2,000 Swedes of proletarian origin decided to move to Brazil in 1890–91. An Italian historian tells us that many of the Italian emigrants simply "abandoned their choice of destination to shipping agents."[16]

Motivated by socioeconomic factors, the volume of migration fluctuated in response to economic conditions on both sides of the Atlantic. And for the same reason, immigrants might change countries or simply return to their native land. Later, we shall consider these phenomena chronologically. It is obvious that if the promise of the agents and the authorities of the host country failed to correspond to the reality of everyday life, disappointed immigrants would attempt to abandon the region or the country that had deceived them.

Should a peasant fail to reach his personal goal of acquiring his own farm in the New World, by 1890 another possibility offered itself as a result of the availability of rapid, cheap (even free) transatlantic voyages, and the fact of alternating seasonal cycles between the hemispheres. A new movement of agricultural labor began, of workers from Spain and Italy called *golondrinas* (swallows) who journeyed to the Río de la Plata in October—November to take part in the harvest of wheat and fruit, returning to Europe in the month of May, perhaps after another brief stay in the coffee districts of São Paulo. Their net earnings were considerable, in their eyes, and they were still able to perform agricultural tasks in their native countries, where their families had remained. Of course, only upon permanently settling across the Atlantic could the *golondrinas* be considered true migrants. Laird Bergad has also alluded to a *golondrina*-type phenomenon in the case of Cuban sugar production.[17]

It is understandable that the experience of the earliest migrants in a location would have a cumulative effect. Upon learning of the failure of a pioneer, for example, relatives and friends at home would not want to follow in his footsteps. The opposite would be true upon receiving favorable news, perhaps accompained by money for passage. Once able to establish an enterprise in the new country, the emigrant would send for young apprentices, usually relatives, from his birthplace, just as had been done during the colonial period.[18]

In this way, the initiatives of leaders of emigrant groups resulted in the establishment of lasting links at the local level between both worlds. In the case of the French colony of Pigüe, in the southern pampas of Argentina, the early colonists set about recruiting only immigrants from Aveyron, their native province.[19] From another French region, the poor and isolated Barcelonette Valley in Alpine Provence, there was a small but steady migration to Mexico from the 1830s on. In fact, the great majority of French immigrants in Mexico up to the Revolution were "Barcelonettes." In Europe they had been peddlers selling textiles from their region in neighboring countries. In Mexico a good many Barcelonettes became wealthy entrepreneurs, employing their fellow countrymen. Most Barcelonettes were single males but they seldom married Mexican women; instead, the reemigration rate was very high. Thus, many rich "Mexicains" returned to France to construct lavish homes and spend the rest of their lives on native soil, finally to be buried under stately gravestones. "They left home in order to be able to stay," as local people, fond of paradoxes, put it.[20]

In 1865, Michael Daniel Jones selected for his Welsh colony Chubut, in Patagonia, an extremely isolated site. The successive waves of immigration to Chubut, which reached 2,000 by the First World War, were usually recruited from the same districts in Wales that the first settlers came from. The Welsh adventure, largely successful in socioeconomic terms, also illustrates very well the influence of extra economic factors. Jones had elected Chubut precisely because it was more isolated than other possible locations such as those in the United States. An ardent Welsh patriot, he hoped that in these remote Patagonian lands the language and culture of Wales could be preserved.[21]

As for the banker-philanthropist Baron Maurice de Hirsch, organizer of the Jewish Colonization Association (ICA), the motive was a desire to transform the persecuted inhabitants of the Eastern European ghettos into prosperous farmers. The crisis of 1890 in Argentina created conditions favorable to his grand project, such as a decline in the price of land and the necessity of attracting foreign capital. During the following decade, some 17,000 immigrants of Jewish origin came to Argentina—"the Jewish Gauchos," of the pampas as they were called. Alberto Gerchunoff describes them with justifiable pride in his book of exquisite short stories.[22]

The United States was the chosen land for utopian experiments of all kinds, but such enterprises were not lacking in Latin America either. Such was the case of the Industrial Colony of Saí (Colonia Industrial do Saí), established in 1842 in Santa Catarina, Brazil, in accordance with the ideas of Charles Fourier. To take another example, William Lane, a socialist newspaperman discouraged by the economic crises and strikes in Australia, conceived of an egalitarian colony in Paraguay. In 1893 he attempted to realize his dream with a group of Australians, only to suffer utter failure.[23]

Latin America, like the United States, was also the refuge of those who had been persecuted for religious reasons in their homelands. The Mennonites, for example, members of an old German sect who, because of their refusal to perform military service, were not allowed to live in peace in either Europe or the United States. Yet they found a refuge in Paraguay. The Paraguayans, a warrior people, considered the use of arms more of a privilege than an obligation; thus the diligent Mennonites were exempted from military service, even in the midst of the Chaco War (1932–35).[24] Italian members of another ancient European sect, the Waldensians, had settled in Rosario, Uruguay, in 1856. As late as the 1920s, they still practiced endogamy and spoke their Piedmontese dialect.[25]

Political refugees continued to arrive, even in an era of mass immigration, though they constituted a tiny group. From Europe came a cluster of French militants after collapse of the Paris commune in 1871, and a group of Germans escaping the antisocialist laws of Bismarck, as well as a number of Italian Anarchists.[26] Less colorful, perhaps, but more numerous were some 10,000 ex-Confederates from the United States who fled to Latin America following the South's defeat in the Civil War. About 2,000 opted for the slave-based society of Brazil, while an even larger number, roughly 5,000, selected the neighboring Republic of Mexico, where slavery had been legalized anew during the short-lived empire of Maximilian. The majority returned sooner or later to the United States, having reconsidered their impetuous decision. In Brazil they experienced difficulty in establishing the cultivation of cotton, more demanding in its technique than that of coffee, and not compatible with existing forms of slave labor in Brazil.[27] It should be noted that few of these immigrants actually had been plantation owners in the United States. Except for some military officers, more plebeian or "popular" elements from the Old South appear to have predominated. A smaller contingent of ex-Confederates also went to Venezuela.

We have examined the structural conditions leading to mass immigration as well as the motivations of collective groups. But we should not forget the individual imponderables that easily escape statistical definition, and are often lost in discussions such as these. For a young Catalan carpenter, for example, who departed "to make for America" (*hacer la América*) in 1927, it appears that the precipitating events that decided him upon his migration were a quarrel with his mother-in-law and a casually overheard conversation.[28] The unfortunate man did not have the success he desired, however; he returned to Spain only to die humiliated by his hostile family years later. A Syrian who settled in Chile related that one of his relatives was "sent to America as punishment for his incorrigible hobby of raising pigeons." The forced emigrant was not only cured of his seemingly harmless weakness, but moreover became a leading industrialist in his new country.[29] In the case of two young Swedish engineers, it is said that one day in 1905 they selected their destination by impetuously stabbing a pencil at a rotating globe. By sheer chance, then, they came to settle in Peru.[30]

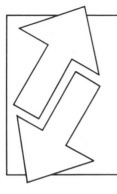

Chapter Four

Mass Immigration
Numbers, Composition,
Distribution, and Function

The Approximate Quantitative Measurement

According to generally accepted calculations, gross intercontinental emigration between 1824 and 1924 comprised a total of 52 million individuals; some 72 percent of these set out for the United States, while 21 percent departed for Latin America and only 7 percent for Australia.

Of the 11 million persons destined for Latin America, fully half—that is, over 10 percent of world immigration, or 5.5 million persons—settled in a single country, Argentina; 5 percent of the Latin American total went to a small neighboring country, Uruguay, while 36 percent settled in Brazil where they preferred to populate the temperate southern regions. This left just 9 percent for all the remaining sixteen or so countries to the south of the United States.

The migratory current arriving in Latin America reached sizable proportions—above 50,000 annually—only toward the end of the 1860s. Immigration to Latin America reached its highest level, some 250,000 yearly, by the mid-1880s, and it sustained these numbers until the First World War. During the 1920s, immigration nearly reached its earlier levels, only to suffer a sharp decline with the Depression of the 1930s (see figure 2).

When using global figures, we should take into account the fact that the various statistics upon which they are based are seriously flawed;

owing to great discrepancies in available quantitative sources. This is the result of administrative deficiencies, as often in the countries of origin as in those of destination, and to migrations occurring by way of second countries, perhaps on both sides of the Atlantic. Then too, there were various definitions of the term "emigrant" by those who recorded the statistics.[1] In Latin America, passengers arriving in second- or third-class sections of ships were generally classified as "immigrants," while in the emigration countries other criteria were used. In Argentina's Río de la Plata region, the immigrant traffic back and forth between Argentina and Uruguay no doubt contributed to the statistical confusion.

In the case of Italian emigration, so important for Latin America, there exist two distinct statistical series commencing in 1902, one based on the number of passports granted to emigrants as established by the Direzione Generale di Statistica (DGS), and the other that of the Com-

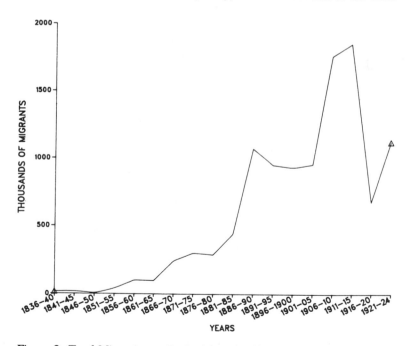

Figure 2. Total Migration to Latin America, 1836–1924
Source: Ferenczi and Willcox (1929, 1:236–37).

missariato Generale dell'Emigrazione (CGE), based on ships' passenger lists. The first, it seems, tends to overestimate, and the latter to underestimate. For Italian immigrants entering Argentina between 1902 and 1914, the difference between both series is 55,333 persons, or about 6 percent. Comparing the two series with the Argentine statistics, the difference between the latter and the Italian DGS (the highest) is 101,179 persons; the Argentine figure is some 10 percent larger.[2] It seems that the principal reason for this discrepancy is that many Italians embarked from French ports.[3] This, at least, is the explanation offered by Mulhall when speaking of Italian immigration at the end of the nineteenth century in South America as a whole. The CGE series includes, to some extent, the Italians who departed from Le Havre, but not those who left from other ports outside Italy.

Between the figures for emigration from the German Empire and

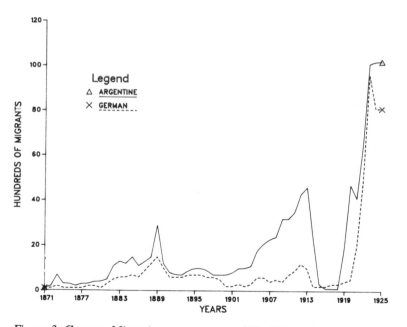

Figure 3. German Migration to Argentina, 1871–1924
Source: Compiled by Laird Bergad and George Calafut, using censuses and compilations published in Argentina and Germany.

those for immigration to the Argentine Republic between 1871 and 1914, the discrepancy is even greater. The Argentine figure exceeds the German calculation by some 43 percent; in this case we may adduce a similar cause, since many German emigrants opted to leave from foreign ports such as Antwerp or Rotterdam (see figure 3).[4]

The discrepancy between the Italian and Brazilian statistics is of a slightly different order. The total of 257,144 Italian immigrants registered in Brazil between 1902 and 1914 is 26 percent lower than the number of Italian passports issued, but 29 percent higher than the number registered on passenger lists. Possibly the excessively high rate of Italian reemigration from Brazil during the period explains this difference.[5] Moreover, George Calafut has pointed to an important Italian administrative change: in 1901 passports were granted free of charge. Perhaps the diminution of the DGS value after this date is explained by the fact that many people got passports who did not use them for emigration. In other instances, we simply lack adequate statistics, as is true for immigration from Spain before 1882.[6]

We should bear in mind that all the figures mentioned until now refer to gross emigration/immigration. It is even more difficult to measure reemigration, even approximately. We know, however, that the rate of reemigration reached a very high level, from 40 to 50 percent, a phenomenon to be discussed later. To take the example of Argentina, between 1857 and 1924, 47 percent of all immigrants appear to have reemigrated. In the Brazilian case, figures are still more incomplete, but they do suggest an even greater reemigration.[7]

The Social and National Characteristics of the Immigrants Entering Latin America

Of the eleven million immigrants who arrived in Latin America between 1854 and 1924, 38 percent were Italians, 28 percent Spanish, and 11 percent Portuguese. The French followed in order with 2.8 percent, the Germans with 2.7 percent, and those designated as "Russians" with 2.6 percent. Italians began to predominate during the 1860s, and continued to do so until 1905, when Spaniards became the most numerous national group (see figure 4).

Of the total Italian emigration between 1881 and 1924, roughly 45 percent left Italy for other European countries; 30 percent opted for the United States, 13 percent for Argentina, and finally, 8 percent for Brazil. And it should be pointed out that until 1890 Argentina attracted more Italians than either the United States or Brazil. Later, Brazil achieved primacy for some years. Between 1900 and 1905, Argentina experienced another increase in Italian immigration, after which the United States became the principal destination for Italians. Since the first waves of transatlantic Italian emigration originated in northern Italy, it is natural that northerners predominated in the South American immigration (representing 60 percent of the Italians arriving between 1876 and 1913). On the other hand, Italians from the south

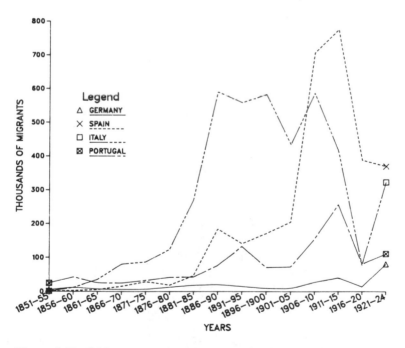

Figure 4. Total Migration to Latin America, by Country of Origin, 1856–1924
Source: Ferenczi and Willcox (1929, 1:262–73).

(mezzogiorno) predominated in immigration to the United States (around 80 percent). It should be noted, nevertheless, that at the same time, if we consider the Italian emigration as a whole (European and extra-European), Argentina attracted a higher percentage of southern than northern Italians (see figure 5).[8]

Qualitative analysis of immigration from Eastern Europe and the Near East is made more difficult by the political and territorial upheavals beginning in the mid-nineteenth century—particularly the dissolution of the three empires of Russia, Austria-Hungary, and Turkey. The persecution of religious and ethnic minority groups did much to stimulate emigration. Driven out by miserable living conditions, ethnic minorities from these areas apparently constituted a high percentage of those labeled "Turks," "Russians," and "Austrians" ("Turks" were Syrians and Lebanese; "Russians" were primarily Jews) who figure in the Latin American immigration statistics before 1914. This is also true of the Irish and Welsh immigrants who often appeared on their passports as "English." Changes in national frontiers can also influence

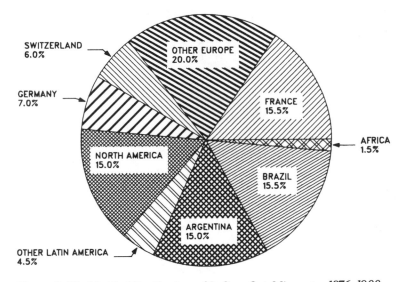

Figure 5. Worldwide Distribution of Italian Out-Migrants, 1876–1900
Source: *Un secolo di emigrazione italiana, 1876–1976* (1978, p. 22, table 3).

the emigration of persecuted groups. In the 1920s, Poland stimulated the migration of the Ukrainian, Bielorussian, and Jewish minorities, while Romania did the same with the Bulgarians and Ukrainians. A specialist on Uruguayan immigration comments: "It is estimated that of the immigrants who arrived [in Uruguay] with Polish or Romanian documentation only about 10 percent were actually that."[9]

About 90 percent or more of the roughly 350,000 migrants from Poland to Latin America between 1869 and 1939 were peasants. One large group met a sad fate: they ended up in Cuba in the 1920s when the United States was their real destination. Emigration agents had mendaciously told them that U.S. entry visas would be easier to get in Cuba than in Poland. Their misery was compounded by the absence of a Polish consulate in Havana or even a priest who knew their language.[10]

As is generally the case, young adults constituted a larger percentage of the migratory current bound for Latin America than either elderly persons or children, and men outnumbered women. Of the immigrants arriving in Argentina between 1857 and 1926, only 29 percent were female.[11] But interesting national differences may be observed. Among the French living in Buenos Aires in 1914, there was a considerable predominance of women. This may have reflected a demand in Buenos Aires for French governesses, seamstresses, and prostitutes. The distributions of age, sex, and marital status would also suffer fundamental changes over the course of time.[12]

Owing to the system of subsidized passages and to the special attraction of Latin America for the Latin countries of Europe, which were also the poorest, the emigratory current destined for Latin America was formed primarily of those from the most deprived sectors of the working class, educationally as well as economically. Among the immigrants above seven years of age arriving between 1908 and 1936 at Santos (the port of São Paulo), some 37 percent were illiterate. Among the Poles only 11 percent were illiterate, while the figure for Spaniards was 65 percent, for Portuguese, 52 percent, and for the Italians, 32 percent.[13] Of all emigrants from the Canary Islands, fewer than 10 percent could read and write.[14] At the same time, Italian immigrants to Latin America, originating primarily in the north of Italy, had overall a higher level of literacy than their counterparts in the United States. But we should note that, nevertheless, the northern Italians who entered Argentina possessed a lower literacy rate than northern Italians who chose the United States, nearly all of whom were literate by the beginning of the twentieth century. This was probably owing to the fact that there were more rural migrants in the Argentine sample (see figure 6).[15]

Without a doubt, people from rural areas predominated in the earliest waves of European emigration to Latin America. To be sure, during that period the rural population was in the majority in the emigration countries. But we should not place too much faith in the statements of the immigrants themselves concerning their former occupations, for they knew very well that those who declared at the port of entry that they were "farmers" would be well received. For example, to receive government-subsidized transatlantic passage to Brazil, one had to be a farmer. Thus the occupational figures derived

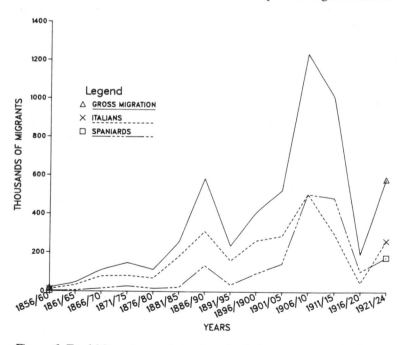

Figure 6. Total Migration to Argentina, the Italian and Spanish Shares, 1856–1924
Source: Ferenczi and Willcox (1929, 1:262–73).

from official sources are not too reliable, based as they are upon personal declarations.

It is clear that more and more immigrants were poor members of the urban proletariat, largely from northern Italy and Spain.[16] Mulhall estimates that of the total Italian transatlantic emigration at the end of the nineteenth century, just 6 percent could be classified as educated persons, 43 percent were artisans and other urban workers, 39 percent agricultural workers, and 12 percent servants.[17]

Just as we observe the proletarianization of the masses of emigrants, we can also notice an opposite tendency among the emigrants from the more rapidly developing countries of northern and western Europe. From Great Britain, Belgium, Germany, Scandinavia, and Poland, numerous technicians and professionals deliberately migrated to Latin America, either because they could not find appropriate work in their own countries, or by the special invitation of Latin American governments. To a degree, European technicians, like the North Americans, were transferred to Latin America in connection with foreign investments. Toward the end of the century, there was an increasing demand in Latin America for technicians and professionals who could assist in the projects associated with economic expansion (railroads, ports, and extractive industries) and general "modernization." Given the antiquated character of the Latin American educational systems, and their limited capacity, this demand was chiefly satisfied by immigrants with specialized training. Recent studies concerning the overseas emigration of Belgian and Norwegian engineers reveal that this was a widespread phenomenon and that Latin America was often the destination. To take an example, all the medical doctors of the Paraguayan army during the regimes of Carlos Antonio and Francisco Solano López were English.[18]

Distribution and Function of Immigration in the Host Countries

More than 90 percent of the total immigration to Latin America was absorbed, as we have seen, by only three of the twenty countries: Argentina, Brazil, and Uruguay. Among the factors that help to explain this concentration are the relatively stable political conditions of these countries, as well as their low population densities, the temperate climates of the regions preferred by the immigrants, and the economic development achieved as a result of immigration itself.

Each Latin American nation exhibited a different kind of immigration pattern. Figure 6 shows that in Argentina between 1856 and 1924, Italians constituted almost 48 percent of the immigrants, while Spanish made up 33 percent. The French were just 4 percent. Fewer Italians came to Brazil between 1851 and 1924 (37 percent), followed by Portuguese (30 percent), Spanish (14 percent), and Germans (4 percent) (see figure 7). In Uruguay, 1881–1924, Italians made up 41 percent of the total immigrants, Spanish 30 percent, and French 6 percent (see figure 8). In Cuba, the predominance of Spaniards continued even after Independence, though a semicolonial master seized the spoils at the end of a bloody struggle with Spain. Spaniards constituted 77 percent of Cuban immigration during the 1882–1924 period (see figure 9). In Chile, on the other hand, between 1882 and 1897 the Spanish, French, and Italian groups each accounted for 21–29 percent of the total, followed by the English and the Germans, each with 6–7 percent. The growing number of "Germans" in the south of both Chile and Brazil owed more to the rapid indigenous growth of isolated population centers than to continuous immigration (see figure 10).[19]

Initially, the majority of the immigrants settled in rural areas, in accordance with their own social origins. In the words of Gaston Gori, the immigrants "arrived with the desire to be farmers, because this was their occupation in Europe." But this was also in conformity with the desires of the host governments, and later, often formed a condition of subsidized voyages. The immigrants concentrated in districts of export production, as renter-producers of wheat in Argentina, or as salaried laborers on the coffee plantations of São Paulo.[20] Gradually, the majority of the rural migrants tended to reemigrate or to move to the great cities, forced to do so by adverse rural conditions. Viewed as a whole, therefore, immigration in Latin America was urban in character. Already by 1895, for example, merely 16 percent of the immigrants in Argentina were employed in agriculture, while 17 percent were artisans or skilled workers, and 14 percent were involved in commerce or transportation. All of these percentages were much higher for immigrants than for the native-born, who were more likely to be domestic servants, day laborers, or unemployed. In 1914, the number of immigrants employed in agriculture had fallen to 10 percent, while that of the natives rose correspondingly. To look at one specific economic sector, that of railroad construction, at times not only had engineers been contracted, but also specialized workers imported from Great Britain, as in the case of the Western Railroad in Argentina in the 1850s. Nevertheless, in building the Central Railroad, during the same years, almost all the workers were Argentine nationals who would be content with less expensive food—that is, meat, abundant on the pampas.[21] The "Russians" continued to be the most rural foreign ethnic group in Argentina in 1914. The great part of them, from the Volga, were of

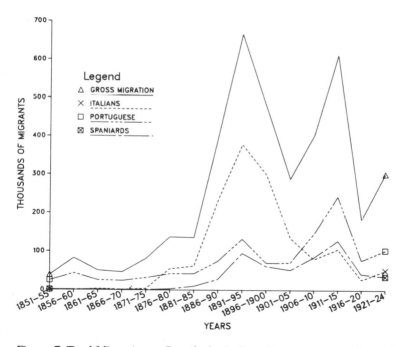

Figure 7. Total Migration to Brazil, the Italian, Portuguese, and Spanish Shares, 1851–1924
Source: Ferenczi and Willcox (1929, 1:262–73).

German descent and spoke German, while others were Jews. Jewish immigrants were predominantly farmers between 1889 and 1905, but later these migrants also moved to the cities, while others came directly to urban areas from abroad.[22]

The various ethnic groups also had distinct characteristics and specializations. In Buenos Aires, Italians were above all retail merchants and construction workers, though many of those from the south of Italy were also peddlers. Basques were frequently milk vendors; and Spanish Galicians, unskilled workers and servants; the French, cooks and teachers; Syrians and Lebanese, merchants—sometimes itinerant. In addition, each ethnic group lived concentrated in distinct neighborhoods within the city; the Italians from the very beginning to the south. In La

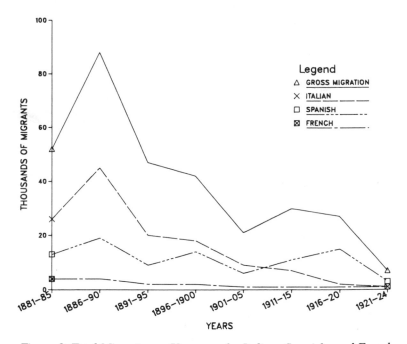

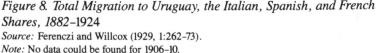

Figure 8. Total Migration to Uruguay, the Italian, Spanish, and French Shares, 1882–1924
Source: Ferenczi and Willcox (1929, 1:262–73).
Note: No data could be found for 1906–10.

Boca, for example, the Genoese exercised a genuine monopoly over river navigation. The Spaniards were even more concentrated in the south, whereas the English and the Germans settled in comfortable neighborhoods to the north.[23]

In Brazil, Germans and their descendants were well known for their rural estates in Río Grande do Sul and Santa Catarina, while the Poles and Lithuanians occupied the same position in Paraná. It should be noted that in the extreme south of Brazil, independent immigrant farmers spread through the forest regions, and were looked down upon by Brazilian ranchers who had settled earlier. The Italians concentrated in the state of São Paulo where they worked on the coffee plantations *(fazendas)* though many held various jobs in cities. The rural districts

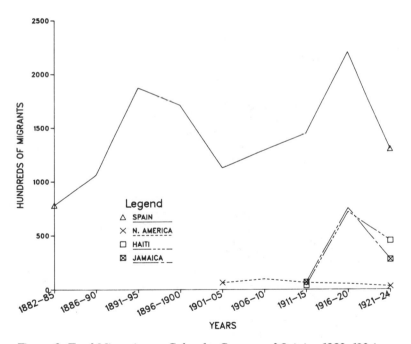

Figure 9. Total Migration to Cuba, by Country of Origin, 1882–1924
Source: For 1882–1900, *Estadística de la emigración e inmigración de España en el quinquenio 1896–1900* (1903, tables 67-68). For 1901–24, Ferenczi and Willcox (1929, 1:525–28).

of São Paulo also absorbed the great majority of Japanese immigrants. In the coffee-growing district of São Paulo, the great *fazendas,* at least for a considerable time, offered nothing more than wage labor. The city of São Paulo was most attractive to the Spanish, while the Portuguese immigrants to Brazil preferred to settle in Rio de Janeiro.[24]

In Peru, a country with much less immigration, migrants usually went into commerce and, as a result, generally lived in the cities. Similarly, the Italian colony in Ecuador, consisting of some 700 persons at the beginning of the twentieth century, was essentially commercial in character.[25] In Santander, Colombia, a small nucleus of German merchants came to control the economic life of the region, notably in the 1870s, by their export of quinine.[26] In Guatemala, Germans became the

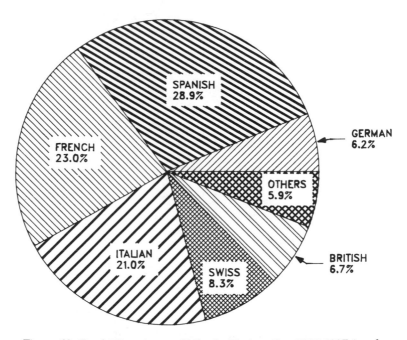

Figure 10. Total Migration to Chile, by Nationality, 1882-1897 (total = 36,510)
Source: Blancpain (1974, p. 481).

principal producers of coffee—an activity dominated by Majorcans and Corsicans in Puerto Rico.[27]

Even within the same rural region in which all the immigrants had settled as farmers, geographical or regional preferences differed among distinct ethnic groups. In Misiones, Argentina, Scandinavians and Germans were to be found in the wooded hills of the interior, while the Japanese elected a site along the banks of the Paraná River and the Poles and Russians opted for flatter, more open lands. Here the bulbous cupolas of Russian churches were raised against the broad and distant horizon.[28]

Factors in the Migration Movement

We have already mentioned some of the "push" factors stimulating mass emigration from Europe. We should now consider other factors that influenced the migratory movement. This is not to say, however, that an adequate explanation exists. Many scholars have fervently debated the relationship between migration from Europe to North America and its economic impact on both sides of the Atlantic without arriving at wholly convincing explanations.[29] In the Latin American case, there still does not exist, to our knowledge, an analysis that embraces all aspects of the question. As a result, we shall only point here to some of the more obviously important circumstances, without limiting ourselves to economic factors, and to note certain details that invite reflection.

Immigration rates fluctuated for a variety of reasons that differed from country to country. German immigrants to Latin America, for example, abruptly dropped from 10 percent of the total in the 1850s, to a mere 5 percent during the following decade. This decline was related to the severe restrictions placed on emigration to Brazil by a decree of the Prussian government in 1859 as a response to the abuses committed against the Germans and Swiss in the *fazendas* of São Paulo. At first, the restriction was limited to São Paulo, but the ban was extended to all of Brazil in 1871. The decree was finally revoked in 1896.[30]

We should note also that total immigration to Latin America fell by 11 percent between 1886–90 and 1891–95, a reduction that clearly reflects the world economic crisis during the early 1890s (see figure 11). It is even more revealing to note that the Argentine share fell from 55 to 25 percent in these years, while immigrants to Brazil rose from 37 to 70 percent of the total. Two important factors help to explain these changes. First, Argentina suffered an acute financial and economic crisis in 1890 that, among other things, provoked the suspension of the subsidized passages that had brought at least 130,000 immigrants to the nation since 1888 (see figure 12). Second, as we have noted, the abolition of slavery in Brazil in 1888 eliminated an important damper on the value of free manual labor. Also, in the late 1880s and early 1890s, because Brazil's economic rhythm was less linked to that of the industrialized nations, Brazil was less affected by the world recession than

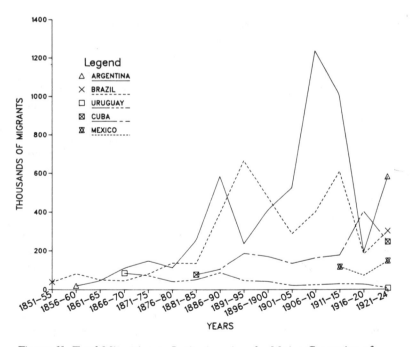

Figure 11. Total Migration to Latin America, by Major Countries of Destination, 1851–1924
Source: Ferenczi and Willcox (1929, 1:262–73).

was Argentina. By 1914 Great Britain was investing fully half of its export capital destined for Latin America in Argentina. Between 1875 and the First World War, a direct correlation developed between Argentine imports of capital goods and foreign immigration.[31]

The state of São Paulo, with the help of the Brazilian government, increased its program of subsidized passages for immigrants to a total of 42 million *milreis* between 1887 and 1904, and thereby attracted almost 700,000 immigrants to the state, mostly Italians. To get an idea of the financial magnitude of this change, we must bear in mind that the value of all the coffee exports through the port of Santos grew from some 36 million *milreis* in 1886 to 74 million in 1887.[32] The program of subsidies itself had been supported, in part, by loans contracted in Great Britain. However, immigration to São Paulo suffered a sharp decline after 1902; in that year 19,311 immigrants arrived as subsidized passengers, but only 229 came in the following year. The Italian government in 1902 prohibited subsidized immigration after learning of the grave abuses committed against the agricultural workers *(colonos)* in the coffee districts of São Paulo. (The Italian government prohibited

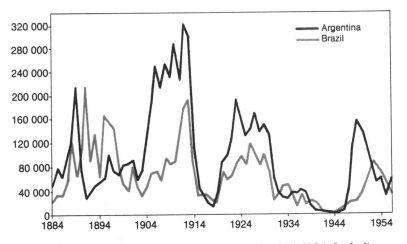

Figure 12. Immigration to Argentina and Brazil, 1884–1954, Including Subsidized Passages
Source: Mörner (1982b, p. 31).

emigration to Argentina in 1911–12.)[33] The government of Spain took the same protective measure in 1911. But the decline in subsidized immigration may also be related to a tendency toward overproduction that began to appear in the Brazilian coffee industry.

In the years of sharpest crisis, the rate of reemigration, always high, actually exceeded that of immigration. In the early 1890s, more foreigners left Argentina than entered it. In 1903, the number of Italians who departed through the Brazilian port of Santos was double the figure for those arriving.[34]

During this period, there was an obvious correspondence between the export of primary products in the state of São Paulo, Argentina, and Cuba, and immigration. The correlation coefficient between immigration and the exportation of wheat from Argentina, in 1871–1910, for

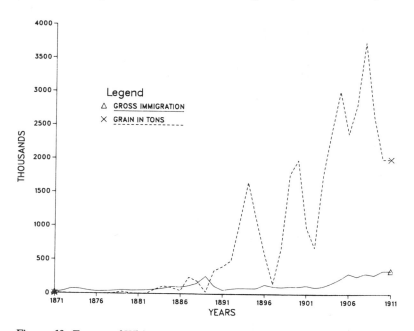

Figure 13. Export of Wheat and Flour from Argentina and Total Immigration, 1871–1910
Source: Scobie (1964, pp. 169–79).
Note: r = 0.8072; r² = 0.6516.

example, was 0.8072. For Cuba, the coefficient obtained in relation to the exports of sugar, during the 1882–1924 period, was somewhat lower: 0.7601.[35] (See figures 13 and 14.) Regarding Brazil, Fernando Bastos de Avila finds a neat correlation between the rise in coffee prices in the port of Santos, and the entry of immigrants into the state of São Paulo, in 1880–1936. (See figure 15.) In addition, this last curve closely follows that of agricultural wages, at least from 1920 to 1936. This contradicts the current idea that wages should fall in a situation of abundant labor supply. Evidently, business trends in coffee exports were decisive factors in these two correlations.

It would be more difficult to establish the impact of the numbers of

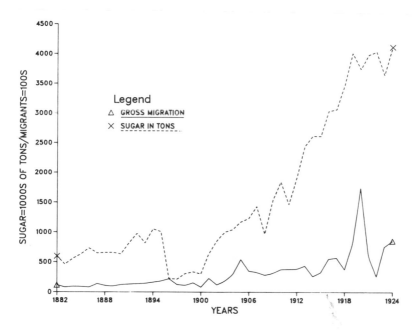

Figure 14. Cuban Sugar Production and Total Migration of Civilians to Cuba, 1882–1924

Source: Thomas (1971, pp. 1562–63). For 1882–1900, Spanish only, see *Estadística de la emigración e inmigración de España en el quinquenio 1896–1900* (1903, tables 67–68). For 1901–24, see Ferenczi and Willcox (1929, 1:523).

Note: r = 0.7601; r² = 0.5778.

arriving immigrants on the volume of production, of course, but no doubt a relationship exists and had a cumulative effect.[36] Political and economic factors are always interconnected. In Chile, a decline in immigration between 1891 and 1908 was related to an economic crisis as well as to the civil war of 1891.[37]

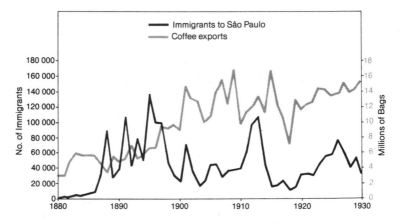

Figure 15. Immigration to São Paulo and Brazilian Coffee Exports, 1880–1930
Source: Mörner (1982b, p. 32).

During the 1911–15 period, the United States came to absorb more than half the world's immigrants (52 percent), while Latin America absorbed just 24 percent. In the postwar era (1921–24, specifically), the total number of immigrants declined from 7,700,000 to 3,600,000 worldwide; but of these, Latin America absorbed a larger share, 31 percent, while the United States share fell to roughly 47 percent. An obvious explanation lies in the fact that the North Americans had begun to impose restrictions on immigration.[38]

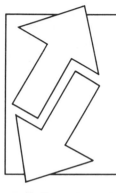

Chapter Five

The Process of Assimilation
Failures and Successes

Many factors determine whether immigrants are assimilated into the culture of a host country, or choose to abandon their new home. Assimilation is related to: (1) the reason for emigration, (2) family ties in the country of origin as well as in that of reception, (3) the conditions, collective or individual, under which they settle in the new country, and (4) nationality.

Among those who emigrated with a commitment to return someday to their native land, many always realized this objective, sometimes returning rich enough to ensure themselves a comfortable old age. They were the *Indianos* of the Mediterranean countries who, after their years abroad, were looked upon by the local population with a mixture of envy, ridicule, and astonishment.[1] Others who left Europe with the same intention failed to return, either because death intervened or because they lacked funds for the return passage or merely had a change of heart—perhaps as a result of unexpected success.[2]

On the other hand, many reemigrated who had not originally intended to return to their homeland. Whatever the precise circumstances, such cases undoubtedly reflected either personal failure or a failure on the part of the host country. Nor should we forget the impact of events in their native lands on those who emigrated.

The rate of reemigration from Latin America came to be quite high, almost 50 percent. Governments were at times disturbed by this phenomenon. The Argentine government in 1911 forced the shipping companies to double the price of return passages to Europe. Although available sources do not permit us to distinguish between the two categories of reemigrants—those who had intended to return and those forced to by failure—this migratory outflow from Latin America compares unfavorably with that of other continents. This point should not be exaggerated, however, for even from the United States, for example, roughly a third of the newcomers reemigrated.[3] Various objective factors help to explain the more extreme Latin American case.

First, we should note the difficulty faced by immigrants—mainly rural people in search of their own land—in attempting to realize their ambition in an agricultural economy dominated by latifundia. In the case of the agricultural workers of São Paulo's coffee-growing areas, it was much easier for them to save the 300 *milreis* for the entire family's return voyage to Europe than to save the 6,000 *milreis* necessary to acquire a small farm.[4] To this fundamental difficulty must be added other adverse circumstances, such as the primitive environment and the rash of diseases to which Europeans were not accustomed, political insecurity, deficiencies in the administration of justice, and the harsh proclivities of the great landlords, habituated as they were to the callous practices of the slave system, toward poor laborers.

Nevertheless, these "objective" factors do not suffice to explain the volume of reemigration, and it is necessary to take into account other personal and subjective circumstances, such as the defeat of the emigrants' hopes raised before departure, and disillusionment in the new country. As we have noted, emigration agencies, encouraged by the Latin American governments and the shipping companies, had played an active role in recruiting migrants by using misleading, even unscrupulous propaganda. When confronted with hard reality in the promised paradise, the immigrants were often sorely disappointed, and decided to return home. Other disillusioned immigrants pursued the search for their "El Dorado" from one location to another, and even from one country to another. Yet exaggerated negative rumors about some Latin American nations also reached Europe; emigrants who had heard them were sometimes able to disprove them by succeeding in spite of adversity, as illustrated, for example, in the letters sent home by Polish peasants who had gone to Brazil.[5]

The marital status of the immigrant could not fail to have an impact on reemigration and assimilation as well. The extent to which an immigrant remained single made reemigration easier; marriage with a native of the new country, on the other hand, greatly favored assimilation. At times, European immigrants founded families with women of a darker color. In the interior of Paraguay, for example, I once met a few Anglo-Saxons and Germans who had taken partners from among peasant women who spoke only Guarani, "going native," as the saying goes. As a result, a new *mestizaje* emerged, but without a significant impact on the local culture. It is easier to find cases in which relatively poor but white immigrants, taken for "gentlemen," succeeded in marrying daughters of the local economic elite. The reemigration of entire families was always more costly, and usually more complicated. However, some immigrant families, especially if they settled within an ethnic community, preserved their separate culture more or less in a closed fashion for generations, especially in an isolated rural environment.

The incidence of reemigration among the diverse ethnic groups from Argentina during the 1857–1924 period is presented in figure 16. We find that 42 percent of the "Russians," 43 percent of the Spaniards, 49 percent of the Germans, 50 percent of the Italians, 53 percent of the French, and as many as 70 percent of the English reemigrated. It is interesting to note, on the other hand, that Czechoslovakians arriving in Argentina between 1922 and 1930 exhibited an exceptionally low reemigration rate, just 8 percent out of a total of 43,000 people. In 1914 the presence of women was higher among the "Russians" who came to Argentina (41 percent) than among either the Spanish (38 percent) or the Italians (37 percent). At the other extreme, women were just 32 percent of the English group.[6] The proportion of women appears to bear an inverse relationship to the rate of emigration for any particular group.

We have already alluded to the fact that cultural affinity influenced the decision of "Latin" peoples such as Spaniards, Portuguese, and Italians to settle in Latin America. No doubt, the same factor facilitated their assimilation, but we should not exaggerate the speed of the process simply because assimilation took place more quickly in Latin America than in the United States. For example, as Mark D. Szuchman has shown, in a provincial urban environment like Córdoba, Argentina, reality often differed widely from the "melting pot" model. It was quite difficult for immigrants to climb the social ladder and most of them soon moved out to try their luck elsewhere. Immigrants turned for protection

to others of their own community. One out of two immigrants in Córdoba, married within the same national group. The continued predominance of marriages between persons of the same ethnicity born in the
new country and/or the preservation of native speech in the home are
examples of the complex vital details that easily escape the grasp of the
social scientist whose work is so often based upon gross statistics.
However, a common national origin did not always assure unity among
immigrants. Italian dialect differences were great enough to warrant the
adoption of Portuguese among Italians in São Paolo as the language of
work outside the home.[7]

Some groups prospered more readily than others. For all the problems they may have encountered, Italian immigrants to Latin America
were often able to improve their situation considerably. This is obvious
if one compares the Italians in Argentina with those in the United

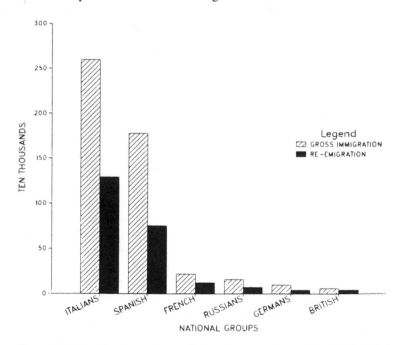

Figure 16. Total Immigration and Reemigration, Argentina, 1857–1924
Source: Ferenczi and Willcox (1929, 1:543–46).

States, as Herbert Klein has done. In Argentina, Italians were the principal immigrant group in acquiring ownership of land, commercial firms, and industries. In the United States, on the other hand, not only the Italian immigrants themselves but also the first American-born generation of Italian descent were mostly reduced to manual labor. The rate of Italian reemigration from the United States was even higher than that for Italians in Argentina. They arrived later in the United States than in Argentina and they found less opportunity and more discrimination there. While those Italians who remained in the United States either sent their savings back home or merely raised their own material standard, those who stayed in Argentina invested more capital in their new country and often moved upward. Klein's hypothesis needs further proof, but it appears more reasonable than the usual theories that stress the predominantly southern Italian origins of the United States immigrants as an explanation for their failure to prosper.[8]

Immigrants from Eastern Europe seem to have been assimilated into Latin American culture slowly but steadily. This occurred, for example, with the Yugoslavs who settled in the most noteworthy foreign colony in the frigid Magallanes in the extreme south of Chile.[9] With respect to the Polish peasants who emigrated to Brazil around 1890, a series of letters written to their relatives in Poland gives an account of their satisfaction. As a matter of fact, these letters failed to reach the folk back home; they were intercepted by Russian censors, which explains why they have survived. No doubt they were seized because of their overwhelmingly positive character. Negative letters, unlikely to inspire other Poles to leave the country, would have been authorized to pass. But, above all, to understand the letters one must take into account the severe misery the emigrants had endured in their native land: "I live much, much better than in Poland, just because I am not subject to any landlord," declared one more or less satisfied immigrant. They found liberty in the forests of the interior of Paraná, but as another observed, "He who desires to eat must work, and he who does not care to work has to return." We should note that Scandinavian immigrants expressed themselves in a similar way during the same era about the North American Midwest, although in their case the levels of hardship both in the place of origin and that in their new home were less severe.

Among the Polish peasants in southern Brazil, the owners of small rural retail stores *(vendistas)* came to play an important role, in Brazilian society. The stores were the centers of both mercantile and social life and the owners sometimes wielded political influence at the local level, as well. The transformation of the immigrants from Poland into Polish-Brazilians was hampered for some time by the prejudice that greeted them in Brazil, but on the other hand, the process was greatly facilitated by their Catholic religion. In fact, religion meant more to the Poles than to the native Brazilians, which should come as no surprise today in light of recent events in Poland. Thus the Polish-Brazilians of a small district in Curitiba, from the 1880s onward, had a much lower percentage of illegitimate children than did the native Brazilians. The continued high marriage and birth rates for the Polish-Brazilians also reflected a more intense Catholicism than that practiced by natives.[10]

In the case of the Germans who settled in the rural areas of southern Brazil and southern Chile, the problem of assimilation proved to be much more delicate. The antiquity of these settlements and their common social institutions militated against their open acceptance of a new nationality. The extraordinary increase in population in these areas occurred in an endogamous situation. In southern Chile, for example, no less than two-thirds of these "Germans," as late as 1917, also continued to live in the same areas as the original colonists. For their part, by 1900 the German-Brazilians of Río Grande do Sul still presented a higher rate of natality (38 per thousand) than that of the state's population as a whole (28 per thousand), or even that of the "old country" during the same era (32 per thousand). In two distinct periods, throughout the last two decades of the German Empire, and again during the epoch of Adolf Hitler, the German authorities attempted to recapture the loyalty of these South American "Germans" for their country of origin, but these efforts had little success. Nor was Benito Mussolini any more successful in attempting to exercise political influence over Italian-Brazilians. At the same time, the two world wars motivated the Brazilian government to apply forced means of assimilation upon the German-Brazilians, some of which were very severe. However, in speaking of the Germans in other Latin American regions, British historian Robin Humphreys cites their "remarkable adaptability," and Brazilian sociologist Emilio Willems cautions us that it would be false to deny that the Germans of southern Brazil achieved a certain level of assimilation.[11]

In the cities, the assimilation of the Germans was a more complex process. In Buenos Aires, the German colony increased from 4,000 in the 1880s to 30,000 in 1914. By 1939 another 15,000 had been added. Until World War II, the elements who were by and large middle class continued to resist assimilation vigorously, while their once considerable economic power and social status declined. Politically, Nazi infiltration was quite successful among them while this was naturally opposed by socialists and Jews.[12]

The group that was most resistant to assimilation were the English; always exclusive, they made matters worse by refusing or finding it difficult to learn Spanish or Portuguese. Historian D. C. M. Platt has described a series of English colonization projects that failed, an outcome he attributes to the fact that an especially high percentage of the colonists were "marginalized urban" people tending toward alcoholism. He also notes that the standard of living of the nineteenth-century English working classes, in spite of all that has been said of their suffering, was better than that of other Europeans during this period. As a consequence, it was more difficult for them to endure the habitual deprivations of the Latin American countryside. On the other hand, a considerable number of very prosperous English immigrants were well ensconced within the economies of the receiver countries. In Argentina, in particular, the English were noted for their sheepraising activities.[13]

The so-called "Turks"—immigrants from Syria and Lebanon, primarily—were assimilated with relative facility, owing in part to their resemblance to southern Europeans. Some adopted Spanish names, either self-designated translations or impositions by immigration employees who did not understand their Arabic names. This would eventually necessitate the publication of guides for the use of the Middle Eastern ethnic communities, to encourage their patronage of Spanish-surnamed Syrio-Lebanese merchants, for example. In 1948 the Syrio-Lebanese community in Mexico conducted a detailed self-survey in order to facilitate this, as well as to learn something of the socioeconomic characteristics of their own group.[14]

With respect to the assimilation of immigrants from the Far East, we can say that in Cuba and Peru the descendants of Chinese "coolies" were remarkably successful in adapting to the new environment, though they suffered greatly in the process—from discrimination and even from violence. From the beginning, the Chinese group was made up almost entirely of single males. On the other hand, Japanese immigration in South America, beginning in 1899, was usually composed of entire families. Their placement was deliberately managed by the Japanese government, and was directed toward the rural frontier areas of Brazil, and the *yungas* of Bolivia. The assimilation of the Japanese immigrants' descendants has been accomplished only in recent times, most commonly in the third generation.[15]

As usual, the immigrants in Latin America were quick to organize associations, especially of the mutual assistance type. However, in a detailed analysis of this theme, Janet E. Worrall comes to the conclusion that in Peru these associations had little importance, especially for the poorer immigrants who depended so heavily on the assistance of relatives and friends. As a result, it would be difficult to arrive at any certain generalization about them.[16]

Within these communities a number of periodicals and reviews appeared in the native languages of the immigrants. The majority of these publications enjoyed a brief life or, at least, a restricted public. Some served to diffuse new ideas, such as *Vorwärts,* published by German socialists, and *La questione sociale* by the Anarchist Enrique Malatesta, both in Buenos Aires. The systematic and comparative study of all these publications would no doubt reveal much of interest concerning the process of assimilation of these diverse immigrant groups, from the nostalgic phase until these ethnic or community voices lost their reason for being, continuing simply as expressions of an ethnicity largely subordinated to national sentiment.[17]

It is obvious that the process of assimilation did not reflect simply the attitudes of the immigrants but also the attitudes adopted by the authorities and the public of the host country. The favorable policy toward immigration of the Latin American governments may be traced to various objectives. Sometimes they reflect on inferiority feeling and a desire on the part of the elite to achieve economic expansion without altering the country's sociopolitical status quo. The very economic success of the immigrants was often a source of suspicion and fear on the part of that same politico-intellectual elite. Nowhere was this more apparent than in Argentina. Unable to cut off immigration which by the time of World War I was viewed as endangering material progress, the elites and competing native social strata enthusiastically turned to defaming the immigrants, and succeeded in doing so, especially the successful merchants of the "Turkish" and Jewish groups. In 1919 a virtual pogrom occurred in Buenos Aires, with at least 150 Jews injured as a result. In the case of Asiatics, the consequences of prejudice were in some cases even worse. In Mexico during the revolution of 1910, the hard-working Chinese immigrants were the object of a bloody persecution in the north that was perhaps worse than the killings that had occurred in California in the late nineteenth century. And the suffering of the Chinese was not limited to the genocidal acts of the Villistas during the revolution. In the northern state of Sonora—which contained the port of entry for most of the Chinese immigrants—violence and, eventually, a complete expulsion, with the loss of all property, resulted in the 1920s.[18]

The defense of the status quo was made all the more evident with respect to certain activist immigrants—anarchists and union organizers, especially. With the purpose of denying them entry or assuring their expulsion, the Argentine government promulgated the so-called Laws of Residency in 1902 and the Law of Social Defense in 1910, modifying substantially, in the process, Argentina's traditional immigration policy.[19] In Brazil there occurred a phenomenon of a distinctly different order. Portuguese immigrants had been viewed there, since colonial times, with envy and repugnance, due in large measure to the material success they had achieved in the cities, and exacerbated by nationalist hostility to the former colonial ruler. Thus, for example, the attempted revolution in Pernambuco in 1848–49 was aimed almost exclusively at the Portuguese. Such xenophobic behavior should be understood in light of the fact that there were no more than twenty-three native Brazilian merchants in Recife at the time, as compared to fifty-four foreign competitors. During the brief civil war of 1893–94, the Portuguese community in Rio de Janeiro was identified with the ill-fated conservative cause, and a violently anti-Portuguese "Jacobin" movement sprang up, supported by the middle class in the Brazilian capital.[20]

However, such hostility did not extend to lower socioeconomic groups. Unlike their United States counterparts, the working classes of Latin America did not manifest such xenophobia, and rivalry with the immigrants was most pronounced among the urban middle class, not workers.

Mass immigration ended, as we have noted, with the Depression of 1930. As a result, today the assimilation of these great masses of new-comers to Latin America is an accomplished fact. The descendants of the immigrants have for some time now been prominent among the spokesmen for nationalism in Latin American countries. Frequently, presidents bear names that are neither Iberian nor even "Latin," and these cases are not limited to Argentina, Brazil, and Uruguay. It is sufficient to recall Lonardi, Frondizi, Livingston, and Lanusse in Argentina, a country in which Carlos Pellegrini was the first president of direct immigrant descent, as early as 1890. In Brazil, one thinks of Kubitschek, Goulart, and Geisel; in Chile, Frei, Alessandri, Pinochet; in Paraguay, Stroessner; in Guatemala, Laugerud. Numerous other cases could readily be cited. Nevertheless, the Latin American nationalism of today is nurtured almost exclusively by traditions that date from the era of Independence, and it does not yet openly recognize the fundamental importance of massive immigration for some Latin American countries during the last century.

Chapter Six

The Impact on
the Host Countries

The importance of immigration for the Latin American nations may be examined in terms of two kinds of results: quantitative and qualitative. It is easier to analyze the first, which involves only a few of these countries—those for which sound data exist and for which the quantitative impact of immigration was of significance.

By 1940, no less than 30 percent of the population of Argentina was born abroad. In the United States, by contrast, the foreign-born never passed the 1910 figure of 14.7 percent.[1] Because most immigrants were of productive age, their reproductive potential was also greater. Thus the demographic contribution of the immigrants and their children to the extraordinary growth of the Argentine population—which increased from some 800,000 inhabitants in 1841 to 14 million in 1940—was on the order of 58 percent. In Brazil, where mass immigration affected only one part of its immense territory, the foreign-born only reached 19 percent. On the other hand, in the state of São Paulo by 1934 immigrants and their children constituted more than half the population.[2] In the city of São Paulo in 1900 there were two Italians for every native Brazilian.[3] In Río Grande do Sul three successive waves of immigrants may be discerned, each with a different ethnic character: between 1824 and 1874, 90 percent were Germans; between 1875 and 1889, 85 percent were Italians; and between 1890 and 1914, 38 percent came from Poland.[4] In spatial terms, Argentina contained an extraordinary concentration of immigrants; in 1914, for example, the capital and the Province of Buenos Aires retained 71 percent of the arriving immigrants. In 1887, Italians alone made up 32 percent of the population of the Argentine capital.[5] In Montevideo, Uruguay, almost one-third of the inhabitants in 1908 were foreigners.[6] The basic importance of mass immigration is clearly reflected in the dynamic population growth of these countries. Between the middle of the nineteenth century and 1903, the population of Uruguay grew almost *thirteen* times, while that of Argentina multiplied *ten* times. In both Brazil and the United States, on the other hand, a less spectacular but nonetheless impressive growth occurred—an increase of five times during the same period. The extraordinary growth of the great population concentrations of the southern cone would not have been possible without the massive assistance of immigration prior to the First World War. In contrast to the powerful demographic impact of immigration on Argentina, Uruguay, southern Brazil, and, to some extent, Cuba, the rest of Latin America was hardly affected by the phenomenon in strictly quantitative terms. There were, of course, many exceptions on the local and regional levels. In 1858, for example, almost a quarter of the population of Lima were foreigners, but it should be pointed out that only half were Europeans.[7]

Looking beyond demographic factors, one quickly observes that the concentration of immigrants in certain occupations considerably increased their impact on the host society. For example, in Argentina in 1895, 81 percent of industrial proprietors, 74 percent of owners of businesses, and 60 percent of blue-collar workers and other employees in industry were foreigners. A look at the lists of employees of two British railroad companies in Argentina from the late 1880s until 1914, shows that only about a third were Argentine, another third were British, and the remainder were other foreigners.[8] Among the workers in the textile industry of São Paulo in 1911, no less than 89 percent were foreigners, and 60 percent of those were Italian.[9] In this manner, the immigrants exercised a profound influence even in those countries in which their demographic percentage was not very high. In Chile, in 1914, only 4 percent of the population was born abroad, and yet immigrants made up 32 percent of the proprietors of businesses and 49 percent of the owners of industrial enterprises.[10] In the Dominican Republic, all tobacco exports, the principal source of foreign trade between 1844 and 1875, were in the hands of a small group of German merchants.[11]

In Mexico, immigrants were rather few but their economic importance, especially during the rule of Porfirio Díaz (1876–1910), was great. In 1880 there were only some 6,500 Spaniards in Mexico, then 16,000 in 1900, and toward 40,000 by 1910. The Spanish were very conspicuous among landowners, merchants, and industrial entrepreneurs. In Puebla, the center of Mexico's textile industry, their presence was especially striking. They owned three regional banks. In Spanish-owned factories, Spanish foremen were loathed by Mexican workers for being harsh and arrogant. But the *gachupines* (as Spaniards had been derisively called ever since colonial times) paid a high price for their power and wealth. In the Revolution of 1910–17, many were killed and their properties sacked or destroyed by the rebels. For all the feuding between the troops of Zapata and those of Carranza, their hatred for the Iberians was the same. Yet Spaniards continued to be prominent as entrepreneurs in the Mexican textile industry until recently when the Lebanese began to supplant them. In the city of Monterrey, near the United States border, immigrants greatly contributed toward making this a great industrial center from the 1890s on. In fact, a few European merchants had laid the basis for this impressive development during the preceding half-century. In 1849, for example, a young Irishman, Patrick Mullins, soon to be known as Patricio Milmo, arrived in the state of Nuevo León. After conveniently marrying the daughter of the governor, Milmo established a virtual empire in ranching, commerce, and banking in the remote areas of Nuevo León. (Incidentally, his own daughter married a Polish prince who inherited the "empire" but had to flee Mexico during the Revolution.) In the mid-nineteenth century, though, a breakdown into "immigrants" and "Mexicans" among the close-knit group of businessmen who ran Monterrey no longer made sense. More important was the fact that, to a large extent, Monterrey's skilled workers, foremen, technical and administrative personnel were Europeans. Even though North Americans formed the most numerous resident foreign group in Nuevo León in 1910, apparently their role in the industrialization of Monterrey was much less significant than that of the Europeans.[12]

The contribution of immigrants, for good or for ill, to the development or underdevelopment of Latin America was much greater than their numbers might suggest. Their presence is intimately related to the agricultural growth of Argentina, Uruguay, Cuba, and southern Brazil; the expansion of manufacturing in Buenos Aires, São Paulo, Santiago de Chile, and many other industrial centers; the professionalization of the armed forces in the principal Latin American countries; and the development of commerce, science, culture, and education in all of the Latin American countries, to name only the most visible results. Obviously, an assessment of the immigrants' contribution in each of these extremely important activities would vary according to the personal criteria of the observer and the moment at which the evaluation were made.

One could regard the impact of immigration in Argentina as having very positive results during the 1930–60 period, when, in spite of numerous problems, the country seemed to be moving toward a better future. However, until very recently that picture has been clouded by a general and profound structural crisis in Argentina. From today's perspective, the political situation has for long remained the most depressing in the older immigration countries, even though recently prospects in Argentina, at least, have brightened.

In consequence, our study of the impact of mass immigration cannot be limited only to its positive, constructive, and tangible effects. Demographic and economic statistics permit one to lapse only too easily into an entirely favorable but one-sided analysis. The tales of personal or group contributions of a positive nature already fill many books—and contemporary "ethnic awareness" and the urge to romanticize ethnic differences could well stimulate many more. But it behooves us to examine as well the impact of immigration in terms of social psychology—to examine the uprooting and alienation of the established middle classes of the great cities clustered around the Río de la Plata estuary, to take an important example. Also, we should inquire whether immigration changed or, on the contrary, reinforced existing economic, social, and political structures in fundamental ways. From the outset, no one would deny that an immense series of changes, large and small, were related to the coming of the immigrants: the introduction of barbed wire (for fences) and other improvements in productive techniques, for example, new modes of eating and dressing, new customs and diversions, and, to no less a degree, a new attitude toward work.[13] But in many other ways, existing negative tendencies in society were reinforced. First, the traditional disequilibrium between the rural areas and the cities became even more accentuated in the course of the twentieth century.

This does not mean, however, that such negative phenomena were directly the "fault" of the immigrants. The responsible factor was the latifundism that predated their arrival, and which presented serious obstacles to their acquiring even moderate-sized tracts of land. The immigrants provided the great landowners, on the other hand, with the labor force necessary to make the elite's empty lands productive. In Argentina, the value of agricultural exports multiplied tenfold between 1870 and 1920. This reflects an even greater extension of the cultivated surface by some 63 times between 1870 and 1914, thanks to the labor carried out by poorly paid immigrant tenant farmers for the enrichment of the landlords. Early or late, most immigrants who had settled in the countryside were forced to abandon the land, choosing to reemigrate or to move to the cities. In this manner, immigration contributed to an exaggerated urbanization and to a monocultural agricultural economy that would soon reveal its weaknesses. In the words of an Argentine historian Cortes Conde, there was, underpinning "the advanced urban Argentina, . . . an almost pastoral society. A parallel industrial development did not exist. When circumstances changed and the external impulse faltered, we discovered that what had been erected was a castle in the air."[14]

Immigration also had a great impact on race relations in Latin America. Reid Andrews's study of Buenos Aires in the nineteenth century, notes that Afro-Argentines were not simply pushed out of traditional "Afro" jobs, such as working as street vendors, fishermen, washerwomen, and porters, by poor immigrants. Rather, blacks and mulattoes, having "absorbed the traditional Argentine disdain for mechanical and manual labor," willingly withdrew into the service sector. Low-level government jobs became especially popular with Afro-Argentines. There, immigrants who were not citizens could not compete with them. Also, mutual hatred often expressed between Afro-Argentines and European immigrants apparently did not prevent a certain degree of intermarriage.[15] The negative impact of immigration upon race relations in São Paulo has been underlined in modern literature; however, this is not to say that the immigrants introduced prejudice and racial discrimination. But by virtue of their great numbers, their education and training, and the preference shown them in the cities, European immigrants quickly replaced black and mulatto ex-slaves in the labor market. Often the immigrants arrived when slavery was on the wane and the ex-slaves were being reattached as "free" laborers on the great plantations. As the immigrants entered the cities, the black freedmen found themselves effectively barred from urban occupations, as Florestan Fernandes has demonstrated in the case of Brazil. Foreigners were hired in their place, with preference going to workers of the same ethnic identity as the entrepreneurs, themselves former immigrants. In the years immediately following the 1889 abolition of slavery in Brazil, freedmen apparently confronted prejudices nurtured, in part, by unflattering comparisons with European immigrants.[16]

It is also evident that in Brazil mass immigration left national and even regional power structures intact. In effect, by providing the elites with a cheap and easily exploited labor force, at a crucial moment—the fall of the empire—immigration inadvertently reinforced the old social structures.[17] In the cases of Argentina, Uruguay, and Chile, a great deal of attention has been paid to the role of immigrants within the political parties. To some degree at the beginning of the twentieth century, they succeeded in changing living conditions as well as political behavior in these nations.

Arturo Alessandri, the famous Chilean statesman, for example, was the son of an immigrant, but as a rule the descendants of immigrants do not appear to have exercised much weight in his party. In Uruguay, naturalized immigrants probably voted for the Colorado party, headed by José Batlle y Ordóñez. In Argentina, we find immigrants well represented within the Socialist party, and, as a result, the object of hostility from members of the Civic Radical Union party.[18] Nevertheless, the tardiness and irresolution that characterized immigrant participation in the political life of the new countries seems much more significant than their active contribution. By 1914, only 2 percent of the immigrants in Argentina had bothered to take out citizenship, and in Chile, in 1895, the percentage of those naturalized was even lower. By comparison, in the United States 46 percent of the foreign-born had been naturalized as of 1910.[19] From the outset, "typical" immigrants, in all countries and during all periods, concentrated on improving their own situation without concerning themselves greatly with politics; they even made an effort to avoid involvement in their new country's political conflicts. In Latin America, it was always dangerous to be concerned with politics, and the immigrants were determined to remain on the margins of these conflicts. Besides, political power was exercised by a small elite until well into the twentieth century, and this too helps to explain the apathy of the immigrants. Of course, this broad generalization admits of many exceptions.[20]

Clearly, the immigrants were pioneers and promotors of what is vaguely called "modernization"; many examples of their contributory role can be cited. Moreover, not a few immigrants achieved notable success in scaling the socioeconomic ladder in their new countries. Perhaps the best known would be the Italian-Brazilian industrialist Francisco de Matarazzo. But in general, upward social mobility for immigrants was much slower, a question of three generations in most cases. It would also be false to attribute all spirit of enterprise and innovation in Latin America exclusively to foreigners. Argentine social scientist Oscar Cornblit stresses the point that the crucial political influence of the immigrant entrepreneurs was limited in the Argentine case, as a consequence of their foreign origins. And as James Scobie has noted, "The self-made man who ascended from stevedore to president of a bank did not exist in Buenos Aires" (in contrast to the possibilities in the United States, and also Brazil, to judge by the case of Matarazzo and others). We should also remember that no small number of Latin Americans sought in Europe and in the United States the training that would place them on the same level as that of the best-educated immigrants.[21]

As we have seen, immigrants were often illiterate upon arrival (with the noteworthy exceptions of the Japanese and, to a lesser degree, the northern Italians) and most of them were accustomed to poverty. Nonetheless, at the outset they represented a sociocultural level somewhat above that of the great masses of population in the receiver countries. The "typical" Latin American suffered from an almost complete lack of instruction. Soon, however, a leveling took place. In 1895, 52 percent of persons born in Argentina were illiterate, whereas only 35 percent of immigrants were. However, this 35 percent illiteracy rate persisted among the immigrants until 1914, while the rate for the native-born had fallen to 39 percent. Many illiterate immigrants learned to read and write in the new country as a result of their own efforts (as was also true of the solitary post–World War II Japanese illiterate who immigrated to Brazil).[22]

Concerning the technology of production, new methods were often introduced into the urban industrial sector but in many rural districts the immigrants simply adopted the rudimentary farming techniques of the area. Again, the Japanese were the exception to the rule. In agriculture, also, we sometimes find foreign-born entrepreneurs introducing modern machines and even steam engines in the nineteenth century to facilitate labor-intensive tasks, such as the hulling of coffee beans in Puerto Rico.[23]

In one respect the contribution of the immigrants to innovation becomes quite clear. We refer to their role in awakening the worker's consciousness, and, concomitantly, in organizing the labor union movement in Argentina, Uruguay, and Brazil. It is instructive to contrast the role played by the Italians in these three countries with that of their compatriots in the United States, where the lack of interest among Italians in unionism was notable. When these immigrants arrived in the United States, workers' organizations had already been formed within a relatively narrow and "moderate" orientation. In Latin America, the same process of labor union formation was largely due to the efforts of the Italian or Spanish leaders (or to natives who were influenced by them), and the resulting labor movement fostered much broader and more radical demands. The anarchism of the Mediterranean world was introduced into Latin America by the immigrants.[24] On the other hand, curiously enough, the mafia of the *mezzogiorno* developed only in the United States.[25]

In reality, whether or not immigrants played an innovative role apparently depended more upon the socioeconomic structure of the receiver country than upon the personal characteristics that the immigrants brought with them.[26]

Viewed from today's perspective, even the contribution of the technocratic and professional elite among the immigrants, so positive at first appearance, becomes to some extent uncertain. The result of these innovations, in a general or long-term sense, may have consisted in the introduction into a somewhat primitive environment of a too costly technology, assuming consumption levels that were too refined and too high. They may also have contributed to reinforcing local dependency upon the foreign technician's knowledge, a psychological dependency so evident in all Latin American countries. According to Richard Graham, there were "so many British engineers in Brazil that the Brazilian image of an Englishman came to be that of an engineer." Eddy Stols observes, however, that technicians from the less powerful countries, such as Belgium, were preferred in the Latin American countries, for obvious political reasons.[27]

Having discussed the impact of the immigrants as workers, technicians, and professionals, we may now ask: what was the role of the immigrants in the process of capital accumulation? In general, immigrants tended to save more of their earnings than did natives. To take just one example, no less than 79 percent of the depositors in the Bank of the Province of Buenos Aires in 1887 were foreigners. But, how much of these savings was returned to the depositor's homeland, with the result that the saving, in itself laudable, became a negative factor for the host country? We know that between 1905 and 1912 the sums sent abroad from Argentina by Spanish and Portuguese immigrants totaled between 50 and 80 million gold pesos. To appreciate the magnitude of this outflow, we should note that the total value of Argentine exports in 1900 was 157 million gold pesos.[28] But it has been shown that at the beginning of the twentieth century, the remissions arriving in Italy from Argentina, Uruguay, and Brazil were much, much lower on the average than those arriving from the United States (despite the lower living standard for the majority of Italian immigrants in North America). It would seem, then, that the Italians of Latin America preferred to invest a major part of their savings in the host country, though we cannot say with certainty whether they did so because it seemed more profitable or because they had arrived at a higher level of integration and identification with the new country. In any case, the remittance of money earned abroad to Italy had a very important impact on the Italian balance of payments in favor of industrialization.[29]

Evidently, deeper, more systematic, and more comparative investigations will be necessary before we can arrive at a balanced understanding of the consequences, good and bad, of mass immigration in Latin America.[30]

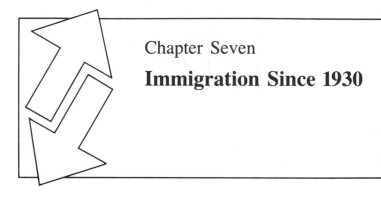

Chapter Seven

Immigration Since 1930

The Impact of the Depression

The worldwide depression of 1929–30 had a violent and profound effect on the Latin American countries by virtue of their heightened dependency during the 1920s on foreign investments and international commerce. Although the Great Depression did not produce in Latin America the massive unemployment suffered by the more industrialized nations, it was obvious that it was no longer meaningful to stimulate mass immigration. Argentina attempted to close its ports to urban immigration between 1931 and 1933, and Uruguay did the same in 1932. Brazil too had decided by the mid-1930s to introduce an ingenious system of quotas that would limit entries. This meant, in practice, that some 27,000 Italians, 23,000 Portuguese, and just 3,500 Japanese would be admitted yearly, for example. Everywhere, governments also opted explicitly for selective immigration.[1]

As a result of the worldwide depression, return migration to Europe took on large proportions. If no jobs could be obtained in the Americas, immigrants felt they had better look for opportunities back home. Thus, for the first time in modern history, in the 1930s Europe gained population through a net in-migration. As a result of this trend and also the flight of refugees from Spain during the Spanish civil war of the late 1930s, France suddenly emerged as the leading recipient of immigrants in the Atlantic world. While all Western Hemisphere countries of this period shared a hostility to immigration, conditions did vary between countries and between regions within Latin America. To these we now turn.

The Argentine case is of particular interest, since Argentina had experienced the largest immigration in Latin America up to the time of the Depression. As a result of the Argentine government's failure to pass legislation securing small landownership in the grain-producing areas, this fertile region was still characterized by "nomadic tenant farming," as R. Paula Lopes has noted. Even in the face of the exodus, as late as 1937, it still proved impossible to achieve land reform through favorable legislation. The failure of all the colonization and land companies, with the single exception of the Jewish Colonization Association, only contributed to the flight of immigrants from Argentina. Speculation in land had been a serious hindrance to potential agricultural settlers through the 1920s, with artificially high land values in the grain-producing areas reaching US$373.00 per hectare by 1929. The price tumbled under the impact of the Depression, however, falling to US$189.00 by 1934—a more realistic figure. But the National Mortgage Bank had halted all loans in 1933.

Only the Jewish Colonization Association functioned by 1936. The reason for its survival may reside in the fact that, alone among the land companies, it had the settlers' interest at heart. The JCA was supported by a philanthropic fund created by Baron Hirsch, whose great desire was to rescue the Jews from the pogroms of Eastern Europe. Its tracts of land were purchased in the 1890s when land prices were low, compared with what they would become in the twentieth century, and the farm plots were distributed to the settlers in a reasonable and systematic manner.

Provincial governments responded individually to the crisis of the 1930s. In Buenos Aires Province, for example, a "Settlement Institute" was established which would serve as an instrument of the planters. But there was no gainsaying the fact that there was a shortage of available land in Argentina in the 1930s. To obtain land, an immigrant needed thousands of pesos in capital, since it was not possible to buy land in installments. The result was an exodus from the countryside to Buenos Aires, or to Brazil where there was plenty of land, or to Europe, which offered the security of family, at least. While in Brazil to the north some urban laborers were abandoning the city to take up rural subsistence farming, in Argentina the flow was entirely the reverse during the depression years.

In addition to this flight to the cities, Argentina suffered massive unemployment in the 1930s. One-third of the labor force lost their jobs. It is not surprising, therefore, that the federal government was forced to abandon its open-door policy by 1931. Regulations were introduced restricting entry for all who arrived as "second or third class or one class passengers" (that is, on immigrant ships). Such persons might enter Argentina only if (1) they were joining relatives already present, or (2) were former residents returning after a brief absence, or (3) were sent for by a settlement already under way, or (4) could show that they held a contract for lease or purchase of land, or finally (5) if they possessed 1,500 pesos. The intent of these regulations is clear: only farmers were welcome, not urban workers—the sector hit hardest by the Depression.[2]

Factories in Argentina, which in 1895 had been almost entirely immigrant-owned, in 1935 were still up to 55 percent in the hands of resident foreigners—discounting those immigrants who had taken out naturalization papers (see figure 17). Oscar Cornblit suggests that this fact largely explains why Argentine governments, following the Depression, paid so little attention to manufacturing and its need for protection.[3]

The result of economic conditions between 1931 and 1935, together with restrictive regulations, was a shift in immigration away from Argentina and in favor of Brazil. Official figures for both countries, admittedly notoriously inaccurate for the period (owing to illegal migration), reveal a net migration to Brazil of 100,000 persons while Argentina apparently received none, since emigration effectively offset immigration. During the Depression years, then, Brazil presents a different case from that of its southwestern neighbor.

Immigration to Brazil also suffered a marked decline during the Depression, but the opportunities presented to settlers in the South were sufficient to stimulate a favorable balance. Between 1880 and 1929, Brazil had received roughly 4,000,000 immigrants, or an annual average of approximately 80,000. During the 1930–35 period, the yearly average declined to less than 17,000. Before the economic crisis, land was granted to settlers on favorable terms and their transportation from

Europe was often subsidized by either the federal or the São Paulo state governments. The regime of Getulio Vargas (1930–45) restricted immigration, however, in response to the demand for urban labor. New laws specified that third-class passengers could enter Brazil only if they were needed for agricultural labor or if they already held a contract or a job. Moreover, all enterprises were now required to have a work force that was two-thirds Brazilian. Exceptions were made in 1931 for mining, farming, and stock breeding—all rural or nonunionized industries.

In the light of nativist and antiforeign agitation during the Depression, the problem of the unassimilated immigrants concerned the

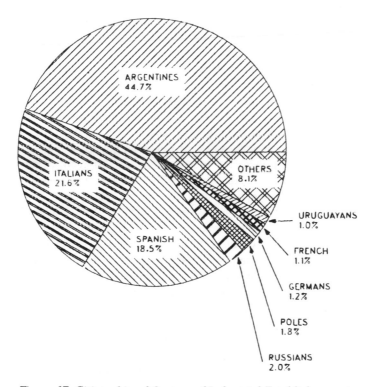

ARGENTINES 44.7%

ITALIANS 21.6%

OTHERS 8.1%

SPANISH 18.5%

URUGUAYANS 1.0%

FRENCH 1.1%

GERMANS 1.2%

POLES 1.8%

RUSSIANS 2.0%

Figure 17. Citizenship of Owners of Industrial Establishments in Argentina, 1935 (total = 52,317)
Source: Cornblit (1967, p. 231).

Vargas government. In 1931 a decree made Brazilian citizens of all who had founded a family in Brazil or had ten years' residence. Several articles in the constitution of 1934 regulated future immigration in an effort to maintain the existing ethnic balance of Brazilian society. Ten years after the United States introduced its national quota system, Brazil did the same. Beginning in 1936, yearly admissions were limited, in theory, to just 2 percent of the official totals for each nationality over the past fifty years. In addition, each entrant was required to furnish proof of employment *(carta de chamada),* plus an invitation from a Brazilian citizen or from the state or federal government. Employees in industry were required to present a contract, which could be renewed, and only agricultural workers were exempted from the additional rule that the immigrant must possess US$120.00 (three *contos*) upon arrival. Perhaps the most demanding requirement was that a Brazilian must guarantee the maintenance and repatriation cost of each immigrant for five years.[4]

By instituting a quota system based on maintaining existing nationality patterns, Brazil was clearly favoring immigration from southern Europe (as surely as a similar system assured the predominance of northern Europeans in the United States). One remarkable result was that in Brazil during the Depression years the southern European quotas were never filled, and the regulations were not strictly adhered to. Enforcement was entrusted to the Ministry of Labor, which chose to calculate the 2 percent based on recent admissions, rather than on settled immigrants. This broadened each national category considerably and by 1936–37 we find that admissions totaled 84,186 persons, or virtually as many entrants as had arrived prior to the new rules. At the port of entry, enforcement tended to be liberally interpreted as well. Officials did not always require the *carta de chamada* but, on the other hand, it seems that agricultural laborers were sometimes driven away by the contract requirements. As a result, Brazilian landowners were unhappy with the new system.

In response, São Paulo state planters and industrialists reacted as they had in the past: they organized the recruitment of European agricultural labor on their own. They welcomed immigrants from Argentina and demanded amendment of the law of 1936. They also encouraged an illegal traffic in *cartas* abroad, and thus undermined the new regulations.[5]

Application of the quota system reflected anti-Asian feeling in Brazil. One apparent result was to demote Japanese immigrants from second position in total yearly arrivals, the rank they occupied in the late 1920s, to a distant fourth place by 1936–37—behind Italians, Portuguese, and Spaniards, in that order. From around 1910 until 1935, large numbers of Japanese farmers had entered Brazil, and they constituted 31 percent of the approximately 271,000 immigrants admitted to Brazil between 1931 and 1935. The Japanese thus became the largest national group to arrive during these economically depressed years, rising to as many as half the arrivals in Brazil in 1933–34; however, by 1939 their share had fallen to merely 5 percent.[6] The Depression unleashed a plethora of hate literature against the Japanese in both Brazil and in Peru, and their immigration was reduced, in part by host government actions. In this manner, Brazilians concerned about the nation's "ethnic identity" were to some extent mollified.

Nothing was done, however, to enforce the constitutional prohibition against the concentration of immigrants in any one part of Brazil. Nor should there have been, for Brazilians proved to be more than willing to move into areas where immigrants congregated—attracted, no doubt, by new economic opportunities there.

Uruguay's situation during the Depression years more closely resembled that of Argentina than that of Brazil. Immigration increased the Uruguayan population until 1931, when heavy departures set in for the first time since World War I. During the years 1919–30, an extraordinary variety in nationality had characterized immigration to Uruguay, as Poles, Serbs, Romanians, people from the Baltic republics, Germans, Austro-Hungarians, Syrians, Armenians, and Jews arrived for the first time. The trend toward reducing emigration in 1931 was followed by a 1932 law restricting immigration on a year-by-year basis. Then, in 1936, a "Law of Undesirables," which became in effect a police law, restricted the entry of working-class immigrants. The economic crisis in the rural areas also contributed to the rapid growth of Montevideo as it fed the outmigration of Europeans.[7]

The Impact of European and Asian Wars

Between 1918 and 1947, Latin America received approximately 288,200 Jewish immigrants, including an estimated 10,000 "illegals." Argentina alone would receive some 120,000 between 1920 and 1947, though it sought to curtail legal entry for Jews after 1923. However, we do not know how many Jews entered Latin America with Spanish passports following Francisco Franco's efforts to rehabilitate them.[8] As Europe drew nearer, step by step, to a new and gigantic tragedy, the Second World War, Hitler's Germany intensified the persecution of the Jews. When the representatives of thirty-two nations gathered in Evian, France, in 1938 to discuss the problem of the Jewish refugees, only one country offered to admit a contingent of as many as 100,000 persons. Paradoxically, that country was the tiny Dominican Republic, autocratically ruled at the time by the dictator Rafael L. Trujillo. With the aid of United States Jewish organizations, the town of Sosúa was established, on the northern coast of Hispaniola, as an agricultural colony in which several hundreds of refugees were settled. For others, the Dominican Republic was merely a stepping stone, a place to pass the time while awaiting a visa to the United States. The motives of dictator Trujillo are uncertain, since he was hardly a humanitarian, but he may have foreseen some profit or personal glory in opening the island to persecuted Jews. It is worth noting also that during the 1880s, another Dominican government, headed by Gregorio Luperón, had attempted to attract a number of persecuted Russian Jews to the island. Perhaps in both cases the desire for white population and the concomitant fear of black Haiti played a role: the Dominican Republic had been by-passed by the mass immigration we have noted in the larger nations of Latin America. In a similar vein, Paraguay also accepted Jews during the darkest days before World War II. The largest contingent of Jewish victims of Nazi persecution was received by Argentina before 1945. While 86,000 Jews entered the country between 1921 and 1935, however, merely another 15,000 were admitted during the crucial years 1936–42. Unfortunately, the Jews experienced much anti-Semitic hostility in Paraguay fomented by local German Nazis.[9]

With the outbreak of the Spanish civil war in 1936, a prelude to the worldwide conflagration, the Mexican government of President Lázaro Cárdenas was quick to demonstrate its solidarity with the Spanish Republicans. After the Spanish government was defeated by the Fascists, Mexico displayed an admirable zeal in attempting to protect the hundreds of thousands of Spaniards who took refuge in France.

Between 1939 and 1942, some 12,000 of these were able to leave France to resettle in Mexico, thanks in part to an agreement between Mexico and the Vichy government. A conspicuous portion of these exiles, some 16 percent, were in the liberal professions. The contribution of this wave of Spanish Republicans to the culture and economy of Mexico was extremely valuable. Another numerous occupational group among the exiled Spanish Republicans were servants (20 percent), and about 40 percent of the emigrants were women. By 1943 almost 30 percent of the exiles had already acquired Mexican citizenship. At the same time, since Mexico refused to recognize the Franco regime, this Spanish American country became the seat of the Spanish government in exile.[10] Additional thousands of Spanish refugees finally settled in the Dominican Republic, among them the author Jesús de Galíndez, later kidnapped in New York and assassinated on orders from Trujillo.[11]

The Postwar Years

By the end of the Second World War, there were hundreds of thousands of refugees in Central Europe who could not or did not wish to return to their home countries, primarily, those of Eastern Europe. Between 1947 and 1950 some 724,000 of these "displaced persons" were transported across the Atlantic. Only 12 percent of them were admitted to Latin America, of whom roughly 37,000 were Jews. One-third of these "displaced" went to Argentina, however, while smaller numbers migrated to Brazil and Venezuela. Nazi war criminals soon appeared in South America, as has been repeatedly demonstrated—the Eichmann case is only the most famous example. Adolf Eichmann, one of the organizers of the genocide carried out by the Nazis against the Jews, escaped to Argentina in 1952 from whence he was kidnapped by Israeli agents in 1960 and transported to Israel to stand trial. Klaus Barbie, who lived in exile in Bolivia until 1983, is a more recent example.

Between 1952 and 1965, another 639,717 refugees were resettled in new countries, according to the Intergovernmental Committee for European Migration (ICEM), but only 4.3 percent of these settled in Latin America.[12] Following the suffocation of the Hungarian Revolution in 1956, another wave of refugees were distributed throughout the Western world, with roughly 1,000 arriving in Brazil. There was also, for example, a good number of Belgian refugees from the Congo (Zaire) who, in 1961, were admitted to Brazil. In 1980, 1,200 refugees from Indochina were allowed to settle in a sparsely populated area in Argentina but were legally prohibited from moving to a town for at least five years, that is, only upon becoming full citizens.[13]

The largest groups of immigrants who established themselves in Latin America during the postwar years were, as before, Italians, Spaniards and Portuguese. We should note, however, that beginning in the early 1960s, the migration of southern Europeans has not been across the Atlantic but instead has occurred within their own country or northward to other European countries because of employment opportunities. However, generally speaking, this northward migration has been less permanent than migration to Latin America before 1960. Between 1961 and 1970, to cite one remarkable example, Switzerland absorbed 1,000,000 Italian workers. During the 1960s a new surge of Spanish emigration began, destined for France, Germany, Switzerland, and other West European countries.[14]

Between 1946 and 1957, as before the Depression, Argentina received the largest number of immigrants in Latin America, a net total of 608,700 persons. After the Second World War, in fact, Argentina appeared to be one of the countries with a splendid future, as it benefited from a favorable economic situation during the first years of the Juan Domingo Perón regime (which lasted from 1946 to 1955). It was not long, however, until economic deterioration set in and this was soon reflected in a reduction of immigration to Argentina (see figure 18).

With the onset of war, the leaders of the Japanese Empire had determined that excess population could not be spared and immigration to Brazil was halted entirely. It was not until 1952 that Japanese emigration recommenced and during the next ten years another 42,631 Japanese were sent to Brazil. Both prewar and postwar Japanese immigration to Brazil differed from its European counterpart in that it was contracted government-to-government, with recruitment both by the government and by private organizations replacing individual initiative. In addition, Japan continued to show considerable interest in the economic activities and well-being of its emigrants long after they had settled in Brazil. Clearly, Japanese economic penetration of Latin

America, which previously had been closed to them, was a primary motive in this policy. The Japanese community in Brazil came to number over 615,000 persons, but immigration slowed considerably in the 1960s, when the booming Japanese economy brought another change of policy; rising wages and a labor shortage at home ended government subsidies and private interest in such a formal arrangement. Japanese immigrants were more likely to be professionals who traveled by air. Japanese-Brazilians came to be concentrated in the states of São Paulo and Paraná, and soon began to move to urban areas, like their European counterparts before them. Many did remain in the countryside, however, where they farmed tiny plots, usually rented, and demonstrated unparalleled success at extracting bountiful crops from the hitherto poorly utilized Brazilian soil.[15]

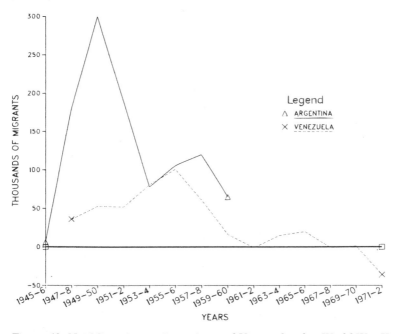

Figure 18. Net Migration to Argentina and Venezuela after World War II
Source: Argentine data cover only movement to and from overseas and Montevideo (Recchini de Lattes, 1969, p. 78). For Venezuelan data, see Suárez (1975, pp. 13, 17).

The total of all immigration to Brazil between 1946 and 1957 was roughly 442,000 persons. Almost half were Portuguese, arriving in especially large numbers during the 1950s. Soon, however, the Portuguese, like the Italians and the Spaniards, found more attractive possibilities in Western Europe. For whatever reason, the official Brazilian attitude toward immigration was more or less negative by 1958.[16]

In addition to the two traditional countries of reception (Argentina and Brazil), Venezuela was also an important destination during the postwar years, as it displayed an exceptionally open immigration policy for the time. A country of low population density, in which a petroleum boom had already led to a rural exodus of alarming proportions, Venezuela imitated its neighbors by attempting to attract diligent European farmers to take the place of those who had abandoned the countryside. This was the same desire that had motivated Argentina, Brazil, and Uruguay, as well as other Latin American countries throughout the nineteenth century. A National Agrarian Institute was placed in charge of the Venezuelan project. Between 1948 and 1957, immigration to Venezuela totaled some 374,000 persons; the country's total population grew by 50 percent during the 1950–61 period, from 5 million to 7.5 million. By 1961, foreigners constituted 15 percent of the economically active population—a high figure for such a recent development. Moreover, 51 percent of the managers of businesses in Venezuela were foreigners, as were 26 percent of the technical personnel.[17]

After the fall of the dictator Marcos Pérez Jiménez, Venezuela passed through an acute economic crisis that gave rise to xenophobic prejudice, as might be expected. The result was a net migration outflow between 1960 and 1962. The tendency toward massive immigration had been stalled, and any hope of repopulating the rural areas remained unfulfilled. Of the 683,000 foreigners who remained in Venezuela in 1963, at least three-fifths had settled in urban areas, 20 percent in the capital, Caracas. Then once again, between 1966 and 1969, there was a net outflow of legal European migrants. At the same time, however, huge numbers of illegal immigrants, mostly from Colombia, helped to fill the still considerable demand for rural labor. In the early seventies, a change in Venezuelan immigration policy took place in connection with the rise in international oil prices and a higher rate of economic growth. In 1976, resident foreigners in Venezuela totaled no less than 1,100,000 people out of a total population of 13,000,000. The largest groups, as shown by figure 19, were Italians, Colombians, and Portuguese. It is worth noting that more than 30 percent were clerical and sales employees, and almost 10 percent professionals. In addition to these resident foreigners, no less than 64,000 had been naturalized in 1973–76, at a much higher rate than previously. A more selective immigration program was implemented in 1976.[18]

As the case of Venezuela illustrates, the new overseas immigration of the postwar period was no longer composed of peasants, or of poor uneducated people, for that matter. The majority of European migrants were educated, skilled, and traveling on their own account with per-

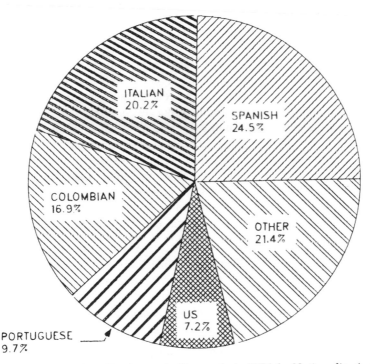

Figure 19. Resident Foreigners in Venezuela in 1976, by Nationality (total = 1,105,800)

Source: Sassen-Koob (1979, p. 464).

sonal funds. They were capable of making significant contributions to the country of their choice. For these very reasons, however, they were also particularly sensitive to adverse conditions, economic or otherwise. Thus there was a high reemigration rate, closely related to economic and political improvements in Europe. Asian immigrants, both before and after the war, on the other hand, had a very small return rate. This was the result of high transportation costs, distance, and the lack of viable options in the country of origin, such as the scarcity of arable land in Japan, for example.

During the 1960s, in most countries, even selective immigration appeared to be losing its raison d'être.[19] It was obvious at any rate that Latin America was caught in an acute socioeconomic crisis, and thus immigration should not be encouraged. The earliest effects of overpopulation could be discerned, at least in certain areas, and massive unemployment and underemployment had become chronic problems everywhere. From the perspective of a spirit of nationalism that was deeper and more sincere than before, it seemed more sensible or realistic to improve the nutrition and the educational opportunities of the rapidly expanding younger generation, than to continue to depend, even to a limited degree, on the influx of "selected" European immigrants. While it is true that immigrants arrived already trained or educated, it was by no means certain that they would remain, and assimilation always required considerable time. Moreover, many Latin Americans began to disabuse themselves of the notion of the superiority of Europeans. However, the old prejudices died slowly. For example, Jesús Arango Cano, a Colombian intellectual, could still write in 1953:

> The three nations of Gran Colombia [Venezuela, Colombia, and Ecuador] urgently need massive white-European immigration, selected from a biological aspect. . . . The eugenetic requirement should be given primacy in the selection of the presumed immigrant [to the end of forming] an American human type that most approximates biological perfection.

Racism also had its expression in legislation regulating immigration in many Latin American countries, usually excluding immigrants from Africa and limiting or attempting to reverse Asian immigration.[20]

In global terms, obviously, Latin America has no further need of increasing its rapidly swelling population by encouraging immigration. On the contrary, as we shall see, today outmigration is a much more important phenomenon. But Latin Americans, naturally, are likely to think in national rather than continental terms and both population density and the rate of population growth, as well as exploitable natural resources, differ widely between the various countries. Thus, Argentina and Bolivia, Uruguay and Guyana are among the few nations in today's world that want to attract large numbers of immigrants for permanent settlement and as a means of increasing their population. But Argentina and Uruguay, for economic and political reasons, saw many more legal migrants leaving than arriving, and Bolivia never proved very attractive. Guyana has an immigration history full of failed schemes, culminating in the revolting, extremely bizarre episode in 1980 when no less than 911 colonists from the United States, following the orders of their fanatic cult leader, committed collective suicide at their Jonestown settlement.[21]

Although the numbers have declined in recent decades, immigrants continue to go to Latin America for a variety of reasons. However, there is another trend, that is, people leaving Latin America. Let us now turn to this countercurrent, and to other, still more important types of migratory movements affecting contemporary Latin America.

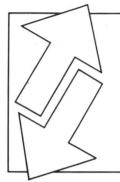

Chapter Eight

Migration from and within Latin America

The Population Outflow

In the early 1980s the outmigration from Latin America has taken on massive proportions and is fed by practically all the Latin American and Caribbean nations. The main destination of emigrants is the United States, but minor currents also find their way to Canada, various European countries, and other parts of the world.

Migration to the United States began as a frontier phenomenon, at the beginning of our century, from Mexico to the U.S. Southwest. The extension of the railroads from central Mexico, with its dense and impoverished rural population, to the north, where mining was booming, paved the way for a further drift of Mexican workers across the border. In 1900, the United States census listed 100,000 Mexican citizens in the border states. By 1910, the figure had almost doubled. Most were farm hands working on a seasonal basis. During World War I, American demand for rural labor increased, while at the same time in Mexico the revolution of 1910-17 caused a large-scale outflow of refugees; the 1920 census takers found almost half a million Mexican-born persons in the United States. The U.S. census of 1930 listed 1.4 million people as "Mexicans" although 600,000 of them were in fact born in the United States. The Depression put a sudden stop to immigration. Within a few years, half a million "Mexicans" had returned across the border, either voluntarily after failing to find jobs or by outright deportation. But soon World War II again raised the U.S. demand for cheap labor. (See figure 20).

In 1942 a *bracero* program, as it was called, was initiated in order to provide Mexican field hands for the North American harvests. In addition, Mexicans were basically seen as replacements for the young men of the United States who had been mobilized as soldiers. This intergovernmental program survived until 1964. Simultaneously, illegal immigration of Mexican workers, called "wetbacks" for having furtively crossed into Texas by wading the Rio Grande (Río Bravo, as Mexicans call it), grew slowly at first, then massively in the 1960s and 1970s, as the "stoop labor" demand peaked, then declined, in the United States. One reason for the fluctuations in the demand for manual labor was the mechanization of agriculture that was proceeding apace throughout North America as a response to rising labor costs. But many farm tasks could be done by machines; moreover, since many post–World War II North Americans

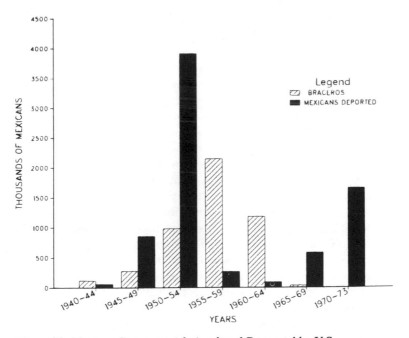

Figure 20. Mexican Braceros *Admitted and Deported by U.S. Authorities, 1940-1973*
Source: Meyer (1975, p. 264); Meyer and Bustamante (1975, p. 296).

found "stoop labor" unrewarding and degrading and the living conditions for workers intolerable, the demand for hand labor persisted. Thus illegal Mexican migrants were often trapped between high unemployment in their homeland and uncertain, degraded employment north of the Río Bravo. Often, the illegal immigrants' children worked in the fields as well—a practice all but eliminated in other economic sectors in the industrial Northern Hemisphere. The plight of illegal migrants was only partially alleviated in the 1960s and 1970s when for the first time U.S. social welfare programs were extended to them in regions where shifting employment needs had the greatest impact.

As opportunities dried up in rural areas, cities such as Chicago and especially Los Angeles accumulated large Mexican populations. These Mexican communities, both urban and rural, like those of the immigrants who had preceded them, were characterized by limited political participation, large families, and sizable pecuniary remissions to relatives abroad. Mexican farmhands without documentation in Oregon told two social scientists some years ago that their gross earnings were six times greater than in Mexico. However, their net income, that is, discounting transportation and higher living costs, was merely three times higher than a Mexican wage.

The numbers of Mexicans apprehended while illegally crossing the U.S. border grew to 150,000 in 1968, and by the late 1970s as many as 750,000 were captured annually, on the average. Many more slipped through the extensively guarded but impossible to secure border region, with its nearly two thousand miles of desert landscape. Many of those captured were repeaters who only days previously had been seized and returned to Mexico following routine processing by the United States border patrol. This population movement became increasingly violent in 1979–80, and residents of both sides of the border began to refer to the region south of Los Angeles as the "battle zone." Mexican-American community organizations resorted to legal action against the border patrol for humiliating treatment meted out to the "wetbacks" by frustrated migration officials. By the 1970s there were well over five million "Chicanos," as the Mexican-Americans were now called, located primarily in the southwestern United States—in the very regions forcibly seized from Mexico more than a century earlier in the war of the 1840s. This heavily Catholic, marginalized, low-income group has begun to develop a notable consciousness of its ethnic identity and potential political power. Like immigrants to Latin America, Chicanos became involved in the trade union movement—in this case, extending to the neglected agricultural sector the kind of labor organization already established in the industrial cities of North America.[1]

To get a better grasp of the nature of Mexican migration to the United States, one should look at its sources. Two social scientists recently studied at close hand a little town called Guadalupe in Michoacán, in central Mexico. Of the 379 households of Guadalupe, three out of four regularly sent migrants to the United States. In 1978, 919 townspeople, almost as many of them women as men, were away in the United States three-fourths of them legally. Almost all migrants sooner or later came back. The people of Guadalupe, according to these researchers, depended heavily on wages earned in the United States, which could represent as much as 79 percent of a family's total earnings. If these statistics are valid, however, Guadalupe must be an exceptional case.[2]

The United States has become the goal of rapidly swelling groups of migrants from all the other Latin American and Caribbean countries as well. There are, for example, no less than 350,000 people from the Dominican Republic concentrated in the New York metropolitan area today. The population of their home country totals 5,500,000. The Dominican migration peaked in the 1960s for economic, not political, reasons; the majority belong to the urban middle class. Between 1958 and 1976 some 114,000 Colombians, also largely middle-class, were admitted to the United States, and the number of illegal entries may have been of the same proportion. As Elsa M. Chaney explains, the increasing immigration from the Caribbean and Latin America is not merely a function of market wage differentials between a large developed country and its less developed neighbors. Ironically, also, even "moderate improvements in economic opportunity in the sending country appear to accelerate the migratory movements since more people can then afford the journey." In one specific case, at least, migration to the United States has been a means of preserving traditional culture and social forms. I refer to the so-called Garifuna, or Black Caribs, the descendants of African slaves and Carib Indians from the islands of St. Vincent and Dominica who toward 1800 settled in Belize and Honduras. Though mostly of African descent, they still cling to their Indian language. As their economic dependence on migratory wage labor has gradually increased, so has the geographical range of their migration. There are now about 10,000 of them in the New York area from where they send remittances to their families back home to enable them to live in their traditional ways.[3]

A highly visible Latin American immigrant group with specific legal status are the Puerto Ricans, who have been freely admitted as citizens of the United States since 1917 as a result of the semicolonial status of the island, a U.S. territory. Between 1947 and 1956, 418,000 emigrated from Puerto Rico to the mainland, and in 1974, there were some 720,000 Puerto Rican immigrants in mainland United States. This is equal to a quarter of the island's population. The immigrants and their descendants, concentrated principally in New York City, now total more than 1,500,000 persons. Since the late 1950s, however, many Puerto Ricans have reemigrated, stimulated in part by problems of racial or ethnic discrimination on the mainland and also by the development of branch plants of U.S. corporate enterprises in Puerto Rico that offer semiskilled job opportunities.[4]

Immigrants from the English-speaking Caribbean were admitted into the United Kingdom for identical reasons. The movement began after World War II when soldiers native to the British Caribbean learned of the possibility of resettling in the United Kingdom. Between 1953 and 1961, West Indian immigrants amounted to some 230,000 persons, leading the British government to reduce this influx drastically in 1962.[5] In a similar way, albeit on a smaller scale, blacks from the French West Indies and Guiana migrated to France; census figures indicate that 65,000 of them were there in 1968. But according to a scholarly estimate there were instead some 150,000 of them in France at the time.[6]

In addition to migrations that are motivated by the hope of material improvement, we should also consider migration for political reasons. Routinely, the frequent political changes that characterize almost all Latin American countries have resulted in the flight of numerous refugees to neighboring South or Central American nations. Following the Cuban Revolution, however, which began in 1959, the discontented opted for a new life in the United States, a country that freely admitted them— partly, it should be acknowledged, from motives of political convenience. Until 1971, when the exodus from Cuba practically halted, this current reached massive proportions, by and large depleting the middle and upper classes of Cuba; significant numbers of workers have also left in more recent years. Concentrated principally in Florida, particularly its southwestern corner, where a colony had long existed, the Cuban-American community swelled to over 600,000 members.

Not merely Cuban natives left the island after the Revolution. In 1953, some 94,000 Europeans and other foreigners lived in Cuba, notably the "ABC" (that is, "Americans," or U.S. citizens, British, and Canadians). With the occasional exception of an Ernest Hemingway, they emigrated along with the Cubans who did not wish to live under Castro's socialism.[7] Then, in the spring of 1980, there was another exodus—the most bizarre, perhaps, in the history of North American immigration— as a result of Fidel Castro's decision to get rid of those he called "antisocial elements." They left first by air, then by boat from Mariel harbor for the United States. This influx resulted from a momentary loss, on the part of the United States, of control over the entry process, when Cuban-Americans contracted boat owners to sail to Mariel and bring Cuban relatives to Key West, Florida. The Cuban authorities insisted that each boat must also depart with people the government wished to see emigrate, in addition to the persons specifically sent for by Cuban-Americans. When this unorthodox immigration, aimed primarily at long-desired family reunification, was forcibly halted by the U.S. authorities by mid-June 1980, preliminary totals for these new additions to the Cuban-American community approached 125,000 persons (which amounted to 1.3 percent of Cuba's population). Most were single males in their twenties, and at least 20 percent were black. It was clear that this was overwhelmingly an emigration of Cuban workers. While their complaints were often political, they also cited low wages, unemployment, scarcity of commodities, rationing, and the success of earlier emmigrants from Cuba as factors influencing their decision to join the "boat lift."[8]

From another Caribbean nation, Haiti, there has also been an exodus by sea. From about 1910 until recently, extreme poverty and overcrowding in the Haitian countryside has caused an outflow of people both to the towns and out of the country, mostly to Cuba and other neighboring countries, and since 1957, political oppression has made life in Haiti even more unbearable for many people. Many Haitians came to the United States after being deported from the Bahamas, another overcrowded

Caribbean nation. Asylum was apparently denied to all of them, a refusal in glaring contrast to the generous treatment accorded Cuban exiles.[9] Even so, it should be noted that, contrary to current ideas, as many as 77,000 Haitians were legally admitted to the United States between 1969 and 1977. Moreover, about a fifth of those in the U.S. work force in the 1960s were professionals and technicians, a share later reduced to a tenth.

In the 1980 "boat lift," 10,000 Haitians set out on the perilous 800-mile voyage to Florida. The first flight by sailing boat was recorded in 1963, and such flights became a mass movement in the 1970s. However, as we have said, the Haitians were less warmly received than the Cubans. The U.S. Immigration and Naturalization Service has tried to disprove their claims that they were escaping extreme political repression rather than harsh economic conditions, but to disentangle political and economic "push" factors would be next to impossible in the Haitian case. It seems clear also that race prejudice and a preference for refugees from communist states are factors in the U.S. response.

Many thousands of Chileans, and other Latin Americans who had taken refuge in the Chile of Salvador Allende's Popular Unity coalition (1970–73), were forced to flee to Argentina, Venezuela, Mexico, and Cuba in the fall of 1973 when Allende was assassinated. But some 20,000 of these were soon forced for political reasons to depart once more for Europe. At present, numerous Chileans, many of them intellectuals, are refugees in Sweden, France, the United Kingdom, and the Federal Republic of Germany. According to statistics supplied by Amnesty International, between October 1973 and September 1976, approximately 18,500 Chilean refugees had been relocated in other countries. While 12 percent settled in Sweden, 9 percent in France and the United Kingdom, respectively, 8 percent in Romania, 6 percent in West Germany, merely 5 percent went to the United States. In addition to these, there were many whose flight, for some reason, was never recorded. Political repression in Argentina and Uruguay, especially, also produced streams of refugees. In Sweden, a country with a liberal naturalization policy, numerous Latin American refugees became citizens after a few years.[10]

The most notable feature of recent Latin American emigration, aside from its frequently political character, is the large percentage of highly qualified persons who leave. Like the earlier immigration of poor workers, this wave of migration is economically motivated: the migrants are attracted by salaries that are much higher than they could make in the "old country," as well as by the potential for regular employment. While the destination is usually the United States, Western Europe, as just mentioned, has also received its share. This "brain drain," as it is often called, usually results from political repression, which is especially severe in Latin American universities. Between 1962 and 1972, according to Ian Rockett, roughly 30,000 South American professionals and technicians resettled in the United States, among them 3,400 medical doctors. Many came from Argentina. Moreover, between 1950 and 1970, roughly 8,000 Argentine professionals and technicians emigrated to the United States.

Against this backdrop, the attempt by the Intergovernmental Committee for European Migration (ICEM) to encourage immigration, already mentioned, is both insignificant and pathetic. The ICEM succeeded in bringing less than 17,000 skilled immigrants to Latin America from 1964 to 1975. The organization also tried to make some of the Latin American professionals return home, but with little success.[11]

The gravity of the flight from Latin American countries cannot be measured by figures alone. The loss of a small cluster of emigrants in a specialized field (for example, the natural sciences) can have a much more negative effect on national development, obviously, than the depature of larger numbers of other professionals such as teachers or medical doctors, who in Argentina, at least, have been overproduced by the universities, in terms of national demand.[12]

An important factor that remains to be investigated is the rate of reemigration to Latin America from Europe and the United States. Both Chile and Brazil, for example, initiated amnesties in 1979–80, which led to the return of many individuals.

Finally, we have to consider the outflow of people from Latin America which is neither economically or directly politically dictated. Between 1947 and 1972, a total of 43,000 Zionist Jews left Argentina and other Latin American countries to settle in Israel in accordance with a main tenet *(aliyah)* of Zionism. Of the Jewish emigrants from Argentina (who represented more than half of all emigrants), 40 percent had settled in kibbutzim, the voluntary agricultural communes, by 1963. If today Jews in Argentina total less than 300,000, this shows a strikingly high percentage of migration for religious reasons, compared, for instance, with figures for North American Jewry. The intermittent outbursts of anti-Semitism in Argentina probably help to explain the phenomenon.[13]

Now that more people are leaving Latin America than are migrating to it, a trend that began around 1960, we may be witnessing a reversal of the earlier massive immigration of the period from the mid-nineteenth century to the Depression of 1930. But it may be premature to suggest such a long-range trend so soon after its appearance.

The earliest large contingents who left Latin America were farmers and workers in search of a living. Among the Mexican *braceros* of 1942–64 we encounter a phenomenon comparable to the Asiatic "contract labor" of the nineteenth century. Rebels and political refugees have always had to cross the borders for temporary safety or for what becomes exile for life. In the nineteenth century and the first half of the twentieth, numerous Europeans sought political refuge in the Americas. In recent decades, such refugees are apt to be Latin Americans who either go north to the United States and Canada or to Western Europe. For some reason, even Latin Americans on the far left are seldom willing to settle in or are welcomed by the countries of Eastern Europe. In recent years we have witnessed the emigration of a professional and technocratic elite in search of better opportunities for employment, as also happened when European elite emigrants went to Latin America decades or even a century ago. Like the immigration that flowed into the Americas before 1930, emigration from Latin America in the future will depend, as far as its volume and composition are concerned, on economic and political fluctuations both inside and outside Latin America. But it seems assured that its magnitude will remain small alongside that truly gigantic phenomenon which is already in movement—internal migration and its corollary, urbanization.

Migration Between Latin American Countries

Migratory movements across the frontiers of the Latin American countries today, like the outflow of Latin Americans toward the United States, is first dictated by wage differentials. Colombian rural workers earn about three times more in Venezuela than in their home country.

Another important characteristic shared by both the movement toward the United States and migration between Latin American countries is that illegal movement is "the dominant type of migration," as a 1982 United Nations study puts it. While the Mexican movement to the United States constitutes the "world's largest illegal flow," in relative terms an even larger proportion of the populations of Venezuela and Argentina are illegal immigrants. Venezuela, with 13,000,000 inhabitants, is estimated to house 2,000,000 illegal aliens, especially Colombians. In Argentina, out of approximately 27,000,000 inhabitants, some 2,600,000 may be illegal migrants. Total migrants moving between the various Latin American and Caribbean nations in 1975 was roughly estimated at 5,000,000 people. In the receiving countries, government attitudes toward this phenomenon vary, depending on labor demand and other considerations. Argentina, with plenty of space, has issued amnesties repeatedly. Venezuela took a similar step in 1980, whereas the Bahamas, with its dense population and meager resources, found itself obliged to take very drastic measures in 1980 toward the many illegal Haitian migrants who had gathered there. In the sending countries, the governments on the whole dislike (or pretend to dislike) emigration but can do little about it. Even extremely crowded Haiti does not promote it.[14]

Such movements of people across borders in the Latin American republics and Caribbean territories also occurred in the past, but on a smaller scale, in both absolute and relative terms. It increased along with the higher level of economic activity after the mid-nineteenth century. When, for example, the North American entrepreneur Henry Meiggs constructed his railroads in Peru, he contracted 25,000 Chilean laborers between 1868 and 1872.[15] Some 150,000 black emigrants left Jamaica in search of work between 1881 and 1921, and more than 30 percent entered the United States before the frontiers were closed. At least as many more opted for Panama to work on plantations and on construction of the canal, while others headed for Costa Rica, just as hundreds still do each year. As far back as the turn of the century, a group of contract workers from Jamaica suffered a hard fate in Mexico during the regime of Porfirio Díaz.[16] About 15 percent of Jamaican emigrants were among the mass of Antillean workers destined for the sugar plantations of Cuba.

The tremendous expansion of the Cuban sugar economy—a tenfold increase of production from 1898 through 1917, at a time when Cuba still suffered from great population losses because of war—was above all facilitated by migrants from Haiti, already the poorest and most densely populated country in the Caribbean. In general, the Haitian workers (contract labor was prohibited in 1902 but continued in practice) returned home after the harvest *(zafra)* but very many remained. Legal migration, 1913–31, reached around 150,000, but the illegal flow was probably on a larger scale. Mats Lundahl estimates a total of almost 450,000 Haitians entering Cuba during the period. Cuban historian Juan Pérez de la Riva estimates that there were 200,000 Antillean blacks in Cuba by 1931. Eight thousand Haitians were sent out of Cuba during the Depression. As late as 1970, 22,500 persons in Cuba were Haitian-born.[17] Haitian peasants also regularly passed to the neighboring, somewhat less miserable, Dominican Republic as seasonal workers. In 1937, between 12,000 and 25,000 illegal migrants from Haiti were cut down by the soldiers of dictator Rafael L. Trujillo. In more recent times, it is said that illegal Haitian migrants caught along the frontier have been rented out to plantations. Characteristically, the Dominican Republic at present imports 9,000–12,000 seasonal workers from Haiti under a bilateral agreement, while it sends its own temporary workers to Venezuela—an illustration of the relativity of low wages.[18]

When the density of population and the opportunities and compensation for work are very different in two bordering countries, migration, legal or illegal, is virtually inevitable. Between 1963 and 1973 almost half a million Colombians, some legally, most illegally, crossed the long border into prosperous Venezuela. Since then, another million Colombians may have followed their example. The very great wage differential between the two countries, even with inflation rates and living costs taken into account, provided the push/pull factors for an overwhelming majority of these mostly very poor migrants. During the 1960s agriculture in Venezuela underwent considerable expansion. At the same time, there was an exodus of rural Venezuelans to Caracas and other cities. Thus the undocumented Colombian migrants filled a virtual void in the countryside. In the course of the 1970s, the Venezuelans tried to promote selective immigration from overseas while at the same time curbing the illegal inflow of unskilled workers along the western border. As a result, in 1976 as many as 48,000 undocumented migrants were deported. The parallel to the problems along the Rio Grande is very close.[19]

Another very dramatic case of migration is that of El Salvador in

Central America, a country with massive unemployment and a population density greater than that of any other mainland nation of the Western Hemisphere (more than 150 inhabitants per square kilometer). Landless Salvadorean laborers migrate into neighboring Honduras, which has only a little over 20 inhabitants per square kilometer, where they cultivate the abundant vacant lands that beckon from afar. Estimates vary as to their numbers, from 100,000 to 300,000. The massive expulsion of Salvadoreans from Honduras and the ensuing war between the two countries in 1969 was a sad testimony to the futility of attempting to find any rational or natural remedy for the problems of human inequality of resources.[20] In recent years, civil war in El Savador has filled camps along the Honduran border with refugees who confront constant danger. Similarly, refugees from Guatemala crowd into Mexico while refugees from Nicaragua, for example many Miskitu Indians, have been compelled to leave their country and take refuge in Honduras.

Argentina, because of its higher wage levels and standard of living, has been very attractive to migrants from neighboring countries, especially Paraguayans, Chileans, and Bolivians (see table 2). During the inter-census period of 1914–47, Uruguayans and Brazilians crossed the River Plate to resettle in Buenos Aires, but most other migrants from the border countries stayed in the Argentine border provinces as rural labor. The Depression cut off overseas immigration—and to some extent, domestic as well—and migrants from border countries could take the places of the Europeans in the industrial and service jobs. The 1947–60 period was one of transition. Out of almost half a million immigrants from border countries in Argentina, more than three-fourths were by 1960 Paraguayans, Bolivians, and Chileans. Most remained to take poorly paid rural jobs. After 1960, the Argentine economic crisis set in and the rate of growth of migration from neighboring countries slowed down. Yet the crisis made such immigrants even more attractive to stagnant enterprises in both the rural and urban areas, because of their willingness to work for low wages. By 1970 almost half of all immigrants from the neighboring countries lived in Buenos Aires. Chileans often settled in Patagonia, and to this group many more were added following the military coup against the Allende government in 1973.[21]

Having discussed migration within and among the countries of Latin America, let us also briefly look at the impact of outmigration on the countries of origin. In Paraguay, with its very low level of development, migration acted as a socioeconomic safety valve, siphoning off a significant part of the swelling population demanding employment, especially the young. Had these young people remained, the ranks of the underemployed would have swelled. Moreover, outmigration appears to have been a political safety valve as well, ensuring the permanence of the Stroessner dictatorship since 1954. Uruguay, with its low natural population increase and very high degree of urbanization, is a very different country. Under the pressure of economic stagnation and, increasingly, political repression, from 1963 through 1975 more than 200,000 Uruguayans left their country. More than half stayed on the other side of the River Plate. In Uruguay, with 2,800,000 remaining in 1975, the already low demographic growth rate has been cut by half (0.5). Moreover, emigrants were largely professionals or skilled workers; thus the actual and potential loss has been great. Finally, as with Paraguay, one cannot

Table 2. Argentine Residents Born in Border Countries, with Percentage Living in Buenos Aires and in the Province of Buenos Aires, 1914–1970

Birthplace	1914	1947	1960	1970
Bolivia	18,256 (3.87%)	47,774 (7.33%)	89,155 (13.74%)	103,700 (36.59%)
Brazil	36,629 (30.44%)	47,039 (32.07%)	48,737 (31.50%)	49,050 (30.38%)
Chile	34,568 (9.29%)	51,563 (16.50%)	118,165 (25.45%)	144,900 (28.78%)
Paraguay	28,592 (11.16%)	93,248 (13.28%)	155,269 (29.61%)	288,350 (58.44%)
Uruguay	88,656 (60.47%)	73,640 (70.47%)	55,934 (74.45%)	58,500 (78.80%)

Source: Carrón (1979, p. 476).

ignore the fact that, regrettably, emigration functions as a political safety valve for a repressive regime.[22]

Inter-Regional Migration

Migrations between different regions within the same country, in general, follow the same pattern as movements between neighboring countries. Usually they have no direct political significance, but the state often tries to promote migration or, alternatively, to prevent it, although such efforts seldom have lasting results. In Colombia, on the other hand, regional migration during the 1950s and 1960s was to some extent a political movement, as Colombians sought to escape from the areas most victimized by civil war and banditry *(la violencia)*.

The colonization of forests, plains, and mountain areas had early precedents during colonial times and the nineteenth century but, on the whole, is a phenomenon of our century. Such colonization in countries like Colombia, Ecuador, Peru, and Bolivia, could not prosper, except in a very limited form, before the elimination of malaria. Some of the recent movements have been spectacular, such as, for example, the emigration from the most developed areas of Venezuela to the province of Guyana. If coolly evaluated, the opening up of faraway areas destined for primary production can prove hard to justify in economic terms, especially in view of the high transportation costs and the need for large-scale investments in highways, bridges, utilities, and other necessities for settlement. Surely, there have been many examples throughout history of pioneer colonization in the wilderness, whether spontaneous (that is, dictated by dire need and poverty in overpopulated areas) or directed and financed, to a greater or less degree, by a national government. More often, however, frontier areas have not been permanently settled at all but have only experienced the sporadic, sudden influx of temporary settlers in response to some boom or the discovery of a new resource.

In the 1970s, the Brazilian authorities made a large-scale attempt to settle the vast reaches of Amazonia. The Transamazon Highway, completed toward the end of the decade, was built to connect northeastern Brazil with the Peruvian frontier (5,400 kilometers). It was hoped that this would enable the miserable peasants and rural workers of the country's traditionally impoverished areas to build a better life in the Amazon basin (instead of filling the slums of southern Brazil's big cities). The ambitious government plan of sending 100,000 families from the northeast as settlers failed, however. Only about 7 percent of the planned total settled along the Transamazon Highway, less than a third of them from the northeast. Organizational problems and obstacles for agriculture explain the failure. Now smallholders continue to drift away while giant ranching interests and land speculation prevail.[23]

Today, most of the inter-regional migration in Latin America, as we shall see, is toward the major cities and the already developed regions rather than toward the uninhabited or sparsely populated areas on the periphery, no matter how much they are acclaimed as the "land of hope" of their country's future.

In various parts of Latin America, the coastal plantation areas have long exerted a powerful attraction for the peoples of the mountainous interior. Migrants who sought work in the coastal areas were often misled by false promises and found themselves trapped in semiservile forms of labor *(enganche)*. In one way or another, since the end of the nineteenth century Peruvians from the sierra have been attracted in large numbers to the sugar and cotton plantations of the north coast. During the 1930s, peasants from Jujuy in northwestern Argentina were distributed among the sugar plantations of Tucumán, sometimes as seasonal workers, and on other occasions as genuine migrants. In all these cases, conditions favorable to a given agro-industrial exploitation were able to alter the ethnic physiognomy of an entire region.[24] We do not possess sufficient data as yet to study these internal migratory movements from the broadest historical perspective, nor do we know enough about migrations occurring before the change in agro-industrial exploitation began in the mid-nineteenth century.

The introduction of mining stimulated migration. We do know of migration from the Peruvian highland province of Aymaráes (Apurímac Department) since colonial times. At that time, Indians were obliged to perform forced labor in turns in the lethal mercury mines of Huancavelica in the central sierra. Outmigration also continued after labor became free, simply because Aymaráes and most of Apurímac are extremely mountainous areas with little cultivable land and as a consequence have almost always been "overpopulated" in terms of available resources.[25]

Climate and geography are factors of fundamental importance to migration, as is illustrated even more clearly in northeastern Brazil, with its extremely inhospitable and unstable conditions. Since the 1877–79 period, and generally at twenty-year intervals, devastating droughts have occurred whose logical consequence is massive emigration. The refugees from the first of these disasters provided workers for the rubber exploitation boom in the Amazon basin as well as the cheap labor required by the cacao plantations along the coast of Bahía. The miserable waves of *flagelados* (the scourged ones) who escaped the drought marched farther south with each twenty-year cycle. The rapid development of the southern region of Brazil made this industrialized zone irresistibly attractive to the human currents from all other parts of the nation. Outmigration from the northeastern state of Ceará, which in 1970 had a population of 4.5 million, totaled around 700,000 between 1872 and 1970.[26]

In Mexico, the constant movement of population from the central plateau toward the central west coast, under way for the last two centuries, has at last begun to decrease. But there was also, from the colonial period on, a steady migration to Mexico City, mostly from nearby districts. As historical demographers Sherburne Cook and Woodrow Borah put it, this occurred "as long as colonial conditions of travel and communication obtained," referring to the quite rudimentary roads and transportation until the 1880s and 1890s. The situation changed when railroad construction made long-distance land travel easier. In recent times, internal migration in Mexico clearly has been directed toward the metropolitan areas. Mexico City received at least 1.5 million internal migrants between 1930 and 1960, and the rate of expansion of small and medium-sized cities was even faster during that period. Between 1960 and 1980, the population of Mexico City skyrocketed from 5 million to 15 million.[27]

The discovery of oil in Venezuela had a dramatic impact. Venezuela was a stagnant and economically backward country in 1900, with little internal migration. But following the petroleum boom that began in 1920, and because of increased life expectancy and hence a population increase, especially after 1940, migrants flocked to the oil fields and crowded into Caracas and its environs. Caracas was booming economically as a result of the growth of petroleum exports.[28]

Rural-to-Urban Migration

With an annual growth rate of 2.6 percent, 1970–80 (down from 2.8 percent during 1960–70), Latin America's population is still growing very fast indeed. The clearest indication of this overwhelming expansion has been, since the middle of the twentieth century, increasing rural-to-urban migration. Between 1960 and 1980, the rural population only grew from 102 to 117 million, whereas the "urban" population (that is, in centers having over 2,000 people) increased from 100 to 228 million during the same years.[29] Measured by this broad criterion, "urban" population climbed from 50 to 66 percent in twenty years.

This division is rather misleading, however, because the small towns with some thousands of inhabitants tend to be closely linked with agriculture and are not very "urban." It appears increasingly more reasonable to reserve the concept of "urban" for concentrations of 20,000 or more inhabitants. With this latter figure as a criterion, the share of the "rural" population of Latin America dropped from 74 percent in 1950 to 55 percent in 1975; city dwellers rose from 26 to 45 percent, almost half the total population. Even though this represents a much lower level of urbanization than in Europe, it is nonetheless much higher than in other parts of the Third World.[30]

The growth of population in the great cities has been even more marked (see map 3). In 1960 there were twenty cities with over a half million inhabitants; by 1970, there were thirty-six, and seven of these had over 2.5 million. During the period of massive migration, Buenos Aires had 1.3 million residents in 1910, while São Paulo had some 400,000 inhabitants. Without massive foreign immigration, Mexico City, the largest Latin American urban entity in the nineteenth century, had reached 400,000. In 1950, Buenos Aires continued to lead, with 3 million, followed by Mexico's Federal District and São Paulo, each with 2 million. In 1970, these three metropolitan areas (extending beyond the antiquated administrative demarcations) each included between 8 and 9 million. By 1980, as we have seen, Mexico City had reached 15 million inhabitants, out of an estimated national population of some 68 million. Thus, one of every four or five Mexicans resided in the Federal District.[31]

The process of urbanization is an intricate one, involving the displacement of large numbers of human beings. These displacements may be

Map 3. *Major Cities in South America in 1980*
Source: Bromley and Bromley (1982, p. 78).

variously defined in terms of the numbers involved and the reasons for their movements, as well as the distances traveled and over what period of time. Recent research enables us to reject many simplistic notions about migration to the cities. First of all, we are not just dealing with a massive exodus of hungry peasants who establish themselves in the "belts of misery" surrounding the great cities in search of any kind of work. Upon closer study, migration to the cities can be seen to entail a series of displacements by the same individual, or a process spanning two or three generations, or a move in several stages, from the agricultural region to the medium-sized provincial city, and from there to the already overcrowded capital. By the same token, these movements involve a very heterogeneous social group. As the percentage of urban population (defined broadly) grows in a given country, the principal conglomerations will naturally absorb a larger and larger proportion of already urbanized people.[32]

The cause of these migrations from the country to the city is, without a doubt, the socioeconomic backwardness of the rural areas in comparison with the development of the great cities. However, according to an Argentine sociologist, the late Gino Germani, the level of rural misery is not necessarily the cause of migration. Emigration reflects a change in mental attitude. Viewed as such, in Germani's opinion, the process of urbanization comes to be a substitute for social revolution.[33] The "push" factors in the rural environment are not limited, nevertheless, to latifundism and other long established evils. The exodus can, on the contrary, accelerate as a result of the modernization of agriculture that reduces the demand for laborers. Nor is it possible to slow the exodus by means of "agrarian reforms" conceived in narrow terms: land with credit, tools, and training. This is no solution. The principal attraction of the cities is the real or illusory promise of work with better pay. For example, James W. Wilkie stresses that in recent years, job opportunities, the level of economic development, and living conditions have been incomparably better in Mexico's Federal District than in the rest of the country.[34]

According to Juan C. Elízaga, those who are clearly unemployed seem to be only a small percentage of the immigrants in the great urban centers.[35] Unlike external immigration, internal migrations to the great cities are composed about equally of men and women. At times women even predominate, a phenomenon that reflects specific employment possibilities for them in the urban environment, as well as the lack of similar possibilities in the countryside. In general, single female migrants come from more nearby districts than do males.[36] Another factor that clearly attracts migrants are the better educational opportunities in the cities, especially for the migrants' children. Nevertheless, recent investigations tend to refute what is usually said about the low level of instruction among the migrants; it seems that in general they possess a higher level of education than was the norm in their place of origin, and one that approaches the average for the place of destination. Thus, the migrant is not necessarily relegated to the least attractive jobs in the urban labor market.[37]

In point of fact, the majority of migrants to the principal conglomerations are themselves of urban origin, that is, they come from smaller cities. As yet, however, we lack historical perspective; nor do we know enough about the phenomenon of rural-urban migration to the smaller cities. It is clear that an important minority of adult migrants to the large cities are not making their first move, whereas others move directly from a rural location to the capital, in accordance with the traditional model.[38] Specialists in urban development warn us against the tendency to exaggerate the relative importance of migration by stages in the course of the same generation. Also unstudied as yet is the rate of return by urban migrants to the countryside. In general, it should be said that it is insufficient to study rural-urban migration only in the areas where migrants have settled. As should always be done in the study of external migration, researchers must also cover the areas migrants have left. the characteristics of the migrant group must be compared with those of the group that remains behind, and the effects of both outmigration and return migration on the community of origin should be duly assessed.[39] For example, the "brain drain" effect—or the phenomenon that those who leave tend to be better educated than those who remain—should be weighed against the value of the skills of those who return to an area.

It turns out to be more difficult than one might suppose to evaluate the contribution of migrants to the demographic growth of the great cities, since this necessitates establishing the differential rates of fertility for both the migrants and the natives of the city. In at least some of the great cities of Latin America, the fertility rates of even the urban residents continue to be very high. According to demographer Eduardo Arriaga who studied Mexico, Venezuela, and Chile in the 1950s, "Migration has not been the principal cause of city growth." Nevertheless, as Richard Morse indicates, during the 1940s internal migration was clearly the principal cause of urban growth in both Mexico and Brazil.[40] In any case, all agree that until the mid-1930s, external immigration had been the principal cause of population growth in Buenos Aires (see figure 21). Since then, and until 1960, this role has corresponded to internal migration. Between 1936 and 1947, almost 40 percent of the indigenous population increase of the Argentine interior was absorbed by the metropolitan areas. During the 1960–70 period, more than half the metropolitan growth of São Paulo, Bogotá, and Lima was still caused by internal migration. (See map 4.)[41] In the case of Mexico City, the principal cause of demographic growth between 1940 and 1950 was internal migration. In Mexico, in more recent times, the rate of migration has come to be greater in large cities of the second rank, such as Guadalajara and Monterrey, than in the capital. In other cases, such as Santiago de Chile, Montevideo, and Lima, the overwhelming size of these capitals is fed by continued immigration.[42]

Rural-to-urban migration reveals parallels as well as differences with the external mass immigration that took place between the third quarter of the nineteenth century and the crisis of 1930. In both cases "push" factors were at work in backward rural environments with undesirable living conditions. In addition, the low level of development of rural Latin America, a principal cause of the present urban immigration, was already instrumental by 1900 in redirecting the majority of European immigrants who had first settled in the country toward the cities. During that period, external immigration resulted in the Europeanization, or the "whitening," of the human scene in the great cities. Today, on the contrary, internal migration is resulting in a darker skin color and a more rural appearance for the great urban masses of Latin American cities. This has given rise to derisive expressions such as *las cabecitas negras* ("little dark heads") that one may hear in Buenos Aires, especially as applied to the darker-skinned *peronista* workers.

There are other more important differences as between these two migrations that are worthy of note. Early in the twentieth century, the Latin American cities seemed to offer almost unlimited possibilities for expansion and for a considerable time the process of industrialization maintained a rapid pace. But in recent decades, the level of industrialization achieved so far no longer offers greater hopes for expanded employment opportunities. Rather, what is occurring is a slowed growth in the urban terciary or service sector, whose percentage of the labor market

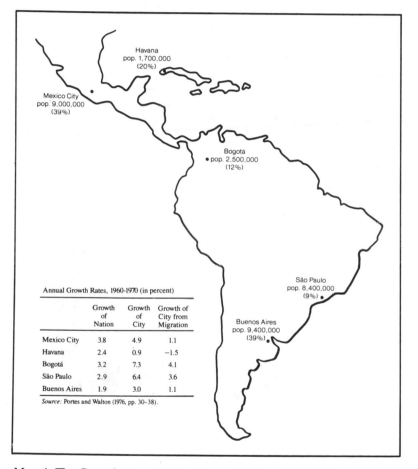

Havana
pop. 1,700,000
(20%)

Mexico City
pop. 9,000,000
(39%)

Bogotá
● pop. 2,500,000
(12%)

São Paulo
pop. 8,400,000
(9%) ●

Buenos Aires
pop. 9,400,000
(39%) ●

Annual Growth Rates, 1960-1970 (in percent)

	Growth of Nation	Growth of City	Growth of City from Migration
Mexico City	3.8	4.9	1.1
Havana	2.4	0.9	−1.5
Bogotá	3.2	7.3	4.1
São Paulo	2.9	6.4	3.6
Buenos Aires	1.9	3.0	1.1

Source: Portes and Walton (1976, pp. 30–38).

Map 4. The Contribution of Migration to the Growth of the Largest Latin American Cities, 1960-1970 (percentage of the total population given in parentheses)

grows ever larger.[43] While the European immigrants once spent no more than a generation in the urban slums *(conventillos,* the Argentine term), today's internal migrants continue to populate the *villas miserias* *(favelas,* the Brazilian word), or "young towns" *(pueblos jóvenes,* as they are euphemistically known in Peru), that grow up without visible improvements, at least in the short run. The casual observer can take hope from the studies of some social scientists who declare that in the long run, say, after ten years on the average, these shanty towns do become stable neighborhoods, equipped with urban services and a better standard of living for the inhabitants. Yet a number of sophisticated studies convincingly lay bare the misery and poverty of the greater part of the Latin American urban environment.[44] At the same time, like cities in the most developed countries, Latin American cities suffer from the

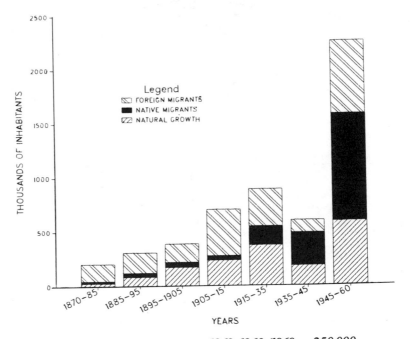

Figure 21. Growth of Buenos Aires, 1869–1960 (1869 = 250,000 inhabitants)
Source: Recchini de Lattes (1971, p. 130).

problems of unmanageable traffic and air pollution—apparently the inevitable companions of urban "progress." Will the inhabitants of the great Latin American urban centers someday be able to bring about the fundamental changes in their economic, social, and political conditions that are necessary to resolve, once and for all, the twin problems of "underdevelopment" and "overdevelopment"? Until now, the poor immigrants of the cities have hardly been more "revolutionary" than their cousins who came from the Old World at the turn of the century.[45] Neither of the two groups has been able to overcome the powerful combination of forces that successfully seem to oppose any radical change in the reality of Latin America's urban life.

It is worth noticing, however, that the two socialist regimes of Cuba and Nicaragua—though, in the latter case, the time perspective is short—have halted the trend toward continued urbanization. The traditional tendency to concentrate budget expenditures, schools, and social requisites in the cities was reversed. The similar tendency by which private capital is invested in urban areas has, naturally, ceased also. The concentration of development efforts in backward, previously neglected rural localities has helped to stabilize the population distribution and rural-urban disparities have been significantly reduced. In Cuba, Havana grew at an average yearly rate of 4.6 percent between 1947 and 1970, expanding even more during the first decade of the Castro regime than before. But the 1970s witnessed a sharp decline in growth to an annual rate of only 1.1 percent, that is, less than half the national rate of population increase, which is relatively low in Cuba. This sharp reversal of the trend toward urbanization during the last decade makes Cuba markedly different from all other Latin American nations. It reflects government policies aimed at strengthening the agricultural sector, but should also be seen against the backdrop of Cuba's economic stagnation.[46]

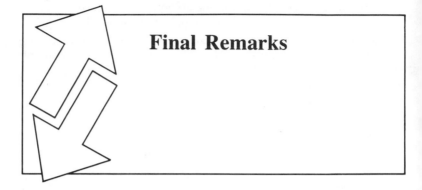

Final Remarks

Until recently, the theoretical discussion concerning migration, as two anthropologists put it, was "time-bound, culture-bound, and discipline-bound."[1] North American students of contemporary migration mostly used microeconomic models emphasizing the role of individual decision making based on the real or imagined comparative advantages of moving versus staying where one has established a home. The migration theory that gradually took shape presumed that the rational calculus of the participants eventually produced an equilibrium in the spatial distribution of the factors of production through the mobility of labor. One is reminded of the "invisible hand" of Adam Smith. Basically, according to this theory, labor moves from where capital is scarce, the labor force abundant, and wages low, to other areas where better conditions prevail. According to the equilibrium model, the mobility of labor will eventually lead to a leveling out of economic growth and human well-being. Within the general framework of functionalist social theory, migration is also often seen as a step toward "modernization," however that vague concept may be defined and understood.

The equilibrium perspective on migration has been increasingly challenged by what is termed the historical-structural mode of interpretation that is largely inspired by Marxism and "dependency" theorizing. Its proponents claim that population movements must be examined in the context of a historical analysis of the broad structural transformations under way in a particular social formation. The perspective is used to lay bare the exploitative relationships that cause both natural resources and the value of human labor to be unequally distributed among the various interests and classes. It stresses conflict instead of harmony, and studies migration as a macro-social instead of an individual process.[2]

It should be noticed that both perspectives are basically grounded in economic reasoning. Noneconomic motives and forces tend to be underrated. Yet the two perspectives differ so profoundly that meaningful communication and intellectual exchange between the proponents of each theory becomes difficult. Neither perspective seems satisfactory to me, yet these contrary points of view can help us to discuss the general themes of our survey of the role of migration in Latin American history.

The Iberian settlement of Latin America during the colonial period, as we have seen, differed from the transfer of enslaved Africans in being a clearly voluntary movement, based on the decision of individuals or households especially with respect to the material advantages of staying or leaving their native country. "Pull" factors seem to have prevailed during the early stage of the settlement process, while "push" factors may have been more important during the later stage. The result was a certain amount of leveling out between the Iberian Peninsula and Luso-Hispanic America. Yet the directing power of the state, underrated by the equilibrium theory, had considerable control over all kinds of migration, both internal and external, during the colonial era, pervaded as it was by mercantilist ideas.

During the early national period, on the other hand, what is striking is the very impotence of the state when, inspired by new liberal values, the Latin countries tried to attract settlers from abroad during a period of adverse economic trends when the situation in Europe was not yet ripe for emigration. Not until the mid-nineteenth century did the profound changes occurring in technology and in the process of production, in combination with population increases, set mass transatlantic migration in motion. In the global vision of Eric R. Wolf, "In the development of capitalism, three waves of migration stand out, each a response to critical changes in the demand for labor, each creating new working classes." The first wave was the short-distance transfer of European peasants to industrial centers in Western Europe where they came to form a working class. The second wave sent Europeans overseas mainly to temperate climates. A third wave "carried contract laborers of diverse origins to the expanding mines and plantations of the tropics."[3] As we have seen, in Latin America, the "third" wave preceded or coincided with the "second" wave. Moreover, the timing of the "third" wave was related to the gradual abolition of slavery.

If we look at Latin America's experience of Wolf's "second" wave, did these massive transfers of people before 1930 contribute to a higher degree of development and balance in the producers of goods, as should be the result according to the equilibrium theory? Or, on the contrary, did they make development more skewed; did they, on the whole, tend to perpetuate the patterns of exploitation, as the historical-structural perspective suggests? The answer to such a highly abstract question will necessarily depend on the area and the historical period one is discussing. Let us limit ourselves to the countries of the southern cone prior to 1950. From that time perspective, external mass immigration, on the whole, led to an improvement in the living conditions of the new arrivals in comparison with those in their countries of origin. It also helped to raise the level of development of the countries of reception.[4] On the other hand, those Latin American countries that remained untouched by mass immigration by 1950 appeared to lag behind. From the perspective of the mid-1980s however, a partly different scene unfolds. We tend to become increasingly aware of the imperfections, indeed developmentally negative aspects, of European immigration to Latin America. As Michael Hall observed in 1974, "Mass immigration in Brazil left the essential structures of power unchanged. In fact, by providing a readily exploitable labor force at a key period, immigration may even have strengthened such structure."[5] Social inequalities were preserved rather than changed as a result of the toil and sweat of immigrant labor. In the long run, as we see it now, it was not so much the immigrants themselves with their ascribed collective "virtues" and "weaknesses" who determined the range and impact of their contribution; rather, the limits were set by preexisting power structures, by the prevailing values. The "melting pot" also took much longer to become a reality in Latin America than scholars used to believe.

Let us turn to Wolf's "third" wave of contract labor in the plantation zones. It is in "Plantation America" that J. S. Furnivall's "plural society" model seems to fit so nicely, with its disjunction into distinctive, mutually antagonistic, hierarchically arranged racial or ethnic segments. But in Wolf's view, such social divisions are not merely evidence of the survival of distinctive traits among the population that are responsible for a bewildering heterogeneity. Instead, in line with historical-structural thinking, Wolf finds the explanation for the "plural society" in the capitalist organization of labor. Naturally, capitalists "did not create all the distinctions of ethnicity and race that function to set off categories of workers from one another," but were able to exploit them profitably. Logically, segmentation should then vanish under socialism, but this, surely, remains to be seen.[6]

The overall picture of migration in Latin America has become infinitely more complex in the twentieth century than it ever was before. Political factors, largely disregarded by both the equilibrium and the historical-structural theorists, have appeared as prime movers. Wars in Europe as well as post-Depression violence in Latin America, notoriously difficult to analyze in clear-cut terms of class conflict unleashed or, at any rate, increased migration. Wage labor migrants have not only crossed national borders within Latin America and the Caribbean but also have emigrated to the United States and Western Europe. But can their movements be satisfactorily analyzed within the micro-economic analytical framework offered by the equilibrium perspective? Surely, sending money to the people back home tends to have the effect of leveling out income gaps. Massive migrations may also help to relieve overpopulation. Yet in the countries of the Third World as a whole, migration not only expresses regional disparities, but also can be seen actually to intensify such inequalities.[7] Migration in Latin America has often served as a socioeconomic safety valve, but no one knows what will happen when it ceases to function as such. What will happen if landless Mexicans have absolutely nowhere to go? What will happen if the jobless are no longer able to leave the increasingly overcrowded Caribbean islands?

On another level, there are the small but highly important currents of professionals and technicians that, in a bewildering way, crisscross the map of the Americas and Europe. Behind this type of migration, swiftly and constantly changing direction, one can perceive not only very cool, businesslike, individual decision making on the part of the migrant, weighing comparative advantages, but also, very often, the impact of political events and other noneconomic considerations that force migrants to move.

Finally, we have to consider the phenomenon of massive rural-to-urban migration, a movement that is in fact less bipolar and less simple to analyze than that expression suggests. Here a very long historical perspective would be appropriate. Urbanization in parts of the Americas even antedated the Iberians, and with very few exceptions the location of the great cities of Latin America was determined in the sixteenth century. After a period of decline in the late seventeenth century, the major centers, in particular, gained new strength a century later. Since the late nineteenth century, urbanization has increased steadily, and expansion has greatly accelerated since the mid-twentieth century. As geographers Odell and Preston put it, so far urbanization is "merely a response to the growth of population in environments whose use by man cannot easily be modified to support more people." At the present juncture, however, in most Latin American countries, the process of urbanization has already exceeded the limits of the rational use of the factors of production. In particular, the superconcentration of people and resources in a few multimillion-inhabitant cities, placing enormous pressure on the environment and natural resources, cannot possibly go on unchecked.[8]

The great advantage of the historical-structural perspective is, of course, that it offers a broad vision of the socioeconomic context in which migration takes place. On the other hand, it has little connection with the infinity of individual human decisions which, whether economically rational or not, are directly responsible for the collective human streams. And the destinations of those streams are largely the result of social networks. Nor can the independent role of, for example, religious factors and sociopsychological phenomena in migration be disregarded. Also, the predictive value of the historical-structural theory appears to be low. At every juncture, its basic assumptions risk becoming outmoded. Thus, for example, as Robert Bach and Lisa Schraml point out, "The attractiveness of immigrant labor to core states and capital has decreased considerably" since the mid-1970s, and the present rapid expansion of the "volume and diversity of global migration" is the result of political rather than economic factors.[9]

Neither the equilibrium theory nor the historical-structural interpretation of migration is adequate to explain the myriad complexities of the subject. However, they may serve as useful oversimplifications, points of departure, from which we can arrive at a more precise analysis of the movement of human populations.

Notes
Bibliography
Index

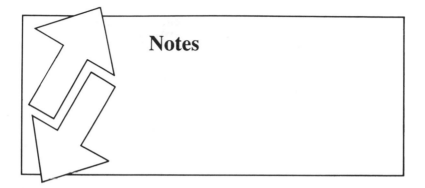

Notes

Introduction

1. Our definition is a modified version of that of Mangalam and Schwarzweller (1970). Compare Lee (1966, p. 49), and Butterworth and Chance (1981, p. 35), who prefer the operational definition of migration as follows: "a permanent or semipermanent change of residence of individuals, families or larger collectivities from one geographical location to another that results in changes in the interactional systems of the migrants." Migration can also be analyzed as an aspect of individual human behavior with the focus on the "time-space paths" of individuals. See Hägerstrand (1969). Köllmann and Marschalck (1980) try to develop a typology of migration connecting the different sets of motives, inducements, forms, and aims of mirgrants to explain whether they are likely to remain or return home. Thus, when an individual's motive is economic, the inducement speculative, the form of migration individual, an immigrant is likely to plan to return. When a group's motive is religious or ideological, the inducement threats and the form of migration that of a community, their aim is to remain, and so forth.
2. The historical significance of the migration phenomenon was discussed at a faculty seminar at the University of Pittsburgh, chaired by Julius Rubin, in December 1976, from which we benefited. For the state of historical research on international migration, see Thistlethwaite (1960), and Åkerman (1975).

Chapter 1. Colonial Antecedents: The Settlement

1. See Mörner (1976, pp. 737–82, 797–804). Legal aspects of migration were studied above all by the late Dr. Richard Konetzke.
2. See, for example, Wolff (1961, pp. 78–108); Campbell (1972); and the excellent recent book by Nunn (1979). According to Boyd-Bowman's sample (1973), on

average, 2.8 percent of overseas migrants licensed by the authorities in Spain, 1493–1579, were foreigners. In 1595–98, (4 percent were foreigners, almost all of them Portuguese (Boyd-Bowman, 1976b, p. 725).

3. Serrão (1974, pp. 105–09); Cardozo (1946). No less than 275 applications of foreigners to be admitted have been found from the eighteenth century, according to Fonseca (1953, pp. 274–75). For an even earlier period, see Stols (1973).

4. Mörner (1976). During 1595–98, the percentage of women increased to 35.3 percent (Boyd-Bowman, 1976, p. 729). See also figure 1. Of the numerous studies which he dedicated to migration, Boyd-Bowman (1973), constitutes the best summary. We also refer to Chaunu and Chaunu (1955–58). See also note 15.

5. Serrão and Pereira (1979).

6. Magalhães-Godinho (1975, pp. 254–55).

7. See, for example, Rodríguez Vicente (1968).

8. López de Velasco (1971, p. xxiv); for the eighteenth century, see Nunn (1979).

9. Consejo Superior de Investigaciones Científicas, *Catálogo* (1940–46); Friede (1952).

10. Boyd-Bowman (1964, 1976a, 1976b, 1976c, and earlier works).

11. Concerning the role of Spanish women in early colonial society, see Lockhart (1968, pp. 150–77), and Burkett (1975).

12. Lockhart (1968, pp. 96–97; 1972, pp. 31–37); Góngora (1969, pp. 79–83); Boyd-Bowman (1976b, p. 729).

13. Mörner (1976, pp. 749–50); Lockhart (1972, pp. 44–52).

14. Ongoing research on the history of women and family structures in colonial Spanish America is very dynamic; we shall soon know more about these issues.

15. Hernández Sánchez-Barba (1961, p. 326). On the other hand, we have various samples for the seventeenth and eighteenth century that permit an analysis of the regional and social composition of migration. We do not know, however, to what extent they lend themselves to generalizations. See Corbett (1974); Antonione, (1965); Brading (1973); Rubio Mañé (1966); Mazet (1976).

16. Mörner (1976, pp. 745f., 779n.56).

17. Mörner (1976, pp. 743, 778n.45); Brading (1973); Socolow (1978, pp. 17, 186f. and *passim*); for a study of some 785 nephews, see Lockhart (1976, p. 785).

18. Brading (1973).

19. Rubio-Mañé (1966). Another sample of immigrant Spaniards between 1595 and 1689 has been analyzed by Mazet (1976, pp. 73–75) in his interesting study of a Lima parish.

20. Mörner (1976, pp. 747–49, 753f.). In a recent study of stratification in Mexico City in 1753, Seed (1982) classifies no less than 81.4 percent of 296 peninsular Spaniards as shopowners and merchants. Another 11.8 percent are classified as "elite" (p. 580). Yet the American-born outnumber the Peninsulars by ten to one in this sample. Thus the Peninsulars constituted no more than 7.4 percent of the "elite" as against 82.0 percent for the Creoles. Shopowners represented 17.2 and

78.1 percent respectively (p. 583). For the religious, see Borges Morán (1977, p. 537).

21. Mörner (1976, p. 769) gives the percentages of foreigners for various population samples of the sixteenth and seventeenth centuries. See also Lockhart (1968, p. 242), Campbell (1972), and Rubio Mañé (1945). For Mexico between 1700 and 1760, see Nunn (1979), who believes that about 12 percent of foreigners were churchmen, 25 percent skilled persons (*mecánicos*), about 25 percent unskilled and another 20 percent merchants (mostly shopowners and the like).

22. See Badura (1971), esp. his three tables; and (1975), on the expulsion (German summary).

23. Magalhães-Godinho (1974, p. 260); Buarque de Holanda (1963, 1: 120–21).

24. For the last part of the colonial period, see Arquivo Nacional (1963).

25. See Otte (1966, 1969); and James Lockhart and Otte (1976). Otte and Albi found a total of 668 letters from Spanish settlers in the "Indiferente" section of the Archives of the Indies. They were added to applications filed by their relatives to enable them also to go to the Indies, often at the cost of the author of the letter. Thus the sample shows a bias in favor of more or less successful migrants. But the same is generally often true in the case of nineteenth-century letters from the Americas, North and South, that have been preserved.

26. Mörner (1976, p. 773f.); Magalhães-Godinho (1975, p. 254).

Chapter 2. The Early National Period: New Beginnings

1. Nicoulin (1973, p. 38).

2. Sánchez-Albornoz (1974, p. 147); text in Bagú (1966, pp. 123–24).

3. Badura (1975a, pp. 79–80).

4. Mecham (1966, p. 228 and *passim*); see also the eloquent letter of the Argentine liberal leader Bernardino Rivadavia in 1818 reproduced by Bagú (1966, pp. 128–31); Berninger (1974, pp. 115–36).

5. Sims (1974b, pp. 34–37). His volumes (1982a, [1985]) deal with the later expulsions.

6. Hernández García (1976). In Venezuela, immigration from the Canaries had been sizable in colonial times. It was resumed in 1832 but in the form of abusive contract labor. In this case, the authorities in the Canaries were instructed from Madrid to stop the emigration in 1859 at a time when the Canarians in Venezuela may have totaled 10,000 people (Rodríguez Campos, 1983).

7. Arquivo Nacional (1960); another two volumes (1961–64) have appeared covering the period until 1842. See also Kellenbenz (1974). While the number of foreign merchants in Rio de Janeiro increased from 57 in 1816 to 91 in 1836, the total numbers of merchants fell from 259 to 215. Thus, the foreigners' share grew from 22 to 42.3 percent (Linhares and Levy, 1973, p. 131).

8. Blakemore (1979). The standard work is Hasbrouck (1969).

9. Paulin (1951).
10. See Anderle (1976), Candido (1976) and Polišenský (1976).
11. Stang (1976); Barros Basto (1970. pp. 41–43).
12. Mörner (1982a, p. 115f.).
13. Duprey (1952, p. 160 and *passim*); Oddone (1966a, p. 59); Martínez Díaz (1978, p. 382).
14. Martínez Díaz (1978, p. 378 and *passim*). On foreigners in the small Uruguayan town of Paysandú in 1833, see Mörner (1982a, p. 107f.); Nicoulin (1973).
15. Griffith (1965). On the Belgian phase, until 1859, see the references in Everaert (1976).
16. Kossok (n.d., pp. 184–96); Brunn (1972, pp. 292–94); Roche (1959, pp. 73–81); Buarque de Holanda (1963, 2:222–30); *RS: Imigração e colonização* (1980, ch. 1).
17. Buarque de Holanda (1963, 2:234–36); on Dona Francisca, see Dall'Alba (1971); Schramm (1964).
18. See above all the great work of Blancpain (1974).
19. Schopflocher (1955).
20. See Herrera Canales, Velasco Avila, and Flores Clair (1981).
21. Schopflocher (1955); Humphreys (1946, p. 52), whose chapter on immigration still constitutes the best summary of the topic. Mulhall (1899, p. 246).
22. Buarque de Holanda (1963, 2:224).
23. Roberts and Johnson (1974).
24. Laurence (1971, pp. 9–10, 17–18).
25. Laurence (1971) provides an excellent survey. See also Sánchez-Albornoz (1974, pp. 150–51); Mörner (1973, pp. 32–33), and the bibliographies to which they refer.
26. Quoted in Pérez de la Riva (1964, p. 89).
27. Stewart (1951); Piel (1974, pp. 87–103); Casey (1975, pp. 145–65).
28. Stewart (1951); Piel (1974); Casey (1975); and Corbitt (1971), esp. figures for the mortality rate in 1847–59 (p. 52). Detailed analysis of Atlantic slave trade mortality is in Klein (1978).
29. Roberts and Byrne (1966–67). See also Adamson (1972), and Engermann and Genovese (1975, pp. 457–73); Weller (1968); Wood (1968); Lier (1971, pp. 217–18); Ankum-Houwink (1974, pp. 42–68); Reyert (1949, p. 241); Nath (1950); Thomas (1974); Schuler (1980).
30. Laurence (1971, pp. 57–62).
31. Conrad (1975).
32. Hernández García (1976).
33. Dean (1976, pp. 88–123), offers the best summary. See also Buarque de Holanda (1963, 2:245–60). The version of the leader of the immigrant "rebels" is given by Thomas Davatz (1972).
34. This section was written by Harold Sims.
35. Brown (1979).
36. Scobie (1971).
37. Oddone (1966b).

38. Oddone (1966b). See figure 8, below. It should be noted that immigration in Uruguay had already reached great proportions at a time when large-scale immigration had not yet set in elsewhere in Latin America.
39. Corbitt (1942). On the Chinese in Cuba, see also Pérez de la Riva (1964, p. 89). For first-hand testimony by the Chinese coolies themselves, see the report of a contemporary Chinese investigative commission, Tsung (1876).
40. Reed (1964). As a result, we find plantations in Cuba at mid-century with a variegated labor force, composed of African slaves, shanghaied Chinese and Mayans, working side by side.
41. Reed (1964).

Chapter 3. Mass Immigration: The European Context and the Selection of Latin America

1. An excellent survey is Oddone (1966a). Statistical data according to the *Cambridge Economic History of Europe* (1965, 4:62). See also Slicher van Bath (1976) and Marschalk (1976). Ferenczi and Willcox (1929) remains the standard work on migrations prior to the Depression.
2. Mosk (1948, pp. 64–66); Bobińska and Galos (1975).
3. Mulhall (1899, p. 534) Carlo M. Cipolla (1973, 2:694–97), "Most dramatic of all was the effect of improved steam shipping on the South American route" (Lorenzoni, 1975, p. 14). We have found no other data on prices prior to 1903 (Franceschini, 1908, p. 881).
4. Foerster (1919, vol. 2); Delhaes-Guenther (1973, pp. 351–53); Oddone (1966a, pp. 22–36); Vázquez-Presedo (1971); on conditions in Apulia, see MacDonald (1963–64); see also Åkerman (1975, pp. 13–14).
5. Nadal (1973, pp. 184–97); Oddone (1966, pp. 36–48); Hernández García (1976).
6. Serrão (1974, pp. 119–59); Ferenczi and Willcox (1929, 1:128–29); Hahner (1976, p. 126).
7. Ferenczi and Willcox (1929, 1:129–31; 2:509–11, 521–53); Korolev (1976); Groniowski (1979, pp. 241–56). Groniowski (1972) undelines the agrarian problems behind emigration. See also Bobińska and Pilch (1975, pp. 87, 124, 127).
8. Mulhall (1899, p. 534); Ferenczi and Willcox (1929, 1:128); Nadal (1973, pp. 185–86).
9. See Pike (1971).
10. Scobie (1964, p. 29); Sánchez-Albornoz (1974, p. 161).
11. Scobie (1964, pp. 30–38).
12. Bourdé (1974, pp. 153–56). See also Solberg (1970, pp. 11–15); Scobie (1964, pp. 122–24).
13. Oddone (1966, pp. 46–48).
14. Vázquez-Presedo (1971, p. 623).
15. Hall (1974, p. 183).
16. The best summary is in Oddone (1966a, pp. 86–97). On the agent/priest, see

Lorenzoni (1975, p. 15); Strelco (1975); Korolev (1976). In 1888, a Swiss law restricted the activities of the recruitment agents who by then had 11 principal agents and 402 subagents in the country (Tobler, 1979; Dore, 1964, p. 101). Karin Stenbäck (1973) on Swedish emigration to Brazil is also useful.

17. Scobie (1964, pp. 60–61); Vázquez-Presedo (1971, p. 615); Foerster (1919, pp. 243–44); Platt (1972, pp. 126–27); and Bergad (1976).
18. Kenny (1973, p. 103).
19. Benassar (1976, pp. 174–80; 1977).
20. Gouy (1980).
21. Williams (1975, 1976).
22. Schwartz and Te Velde (1939, pp. 185–203); Scobie (1964, pp. 124–25); Lee (1970, pp. 259–72).
23. Barros Basto (1970, p. 24); Livermore (1950, pp. 290–313).
24. Fretz (1953); Hack (n.d.). The privileges of the Mennonites in Paraguay were set forth in a law of 1921, reproduced by Hack (n.d., pp. 39–40). They first arrived in Argentina in 1877 (Schopflocher, 1955, p. 67).
25. Hugarte and Vidart (1969, 2:40–43).
26. Segall (1972).
27. Buarque de Holanda (1969, 2:261–73). See also Rollo (1965); Hanna and Hanna (1960).
28. Marsal (1972).
29. Chuaqui (1942, p. 174).
30. Rogberg (1954, p. 21).

Chapter 4. Mass Immigration: Numbers, Composition, Distribution, and Function

1. See, for example, Thistlethwaite (1960, pp. 37–38); Sánchez-Albornoz (1974, p. 155).
2. See Carmagnani and Mantelli (1979), a report strongly criticized, in part, by Calafut (1977), whose conclusions are those summarized in the text.
3. Mulhall (1899, p. 695).
4. See also Everaert (1979). On the discrepancies betweeen German and Brazilian figures, see Brunn (1971, p. 143).
5. Carmagnani and Mantelli (1979); Calafut (1977).
6. Hernández García (1979).
7. Sánchez-Albornoz (1974, p. 158, table).
8. Baily (1969, 1970, p. 127); Calafut (1977).
9. Åkerman (1975, pp. 41–43).
10. Smolana (1983); Kula (1983). The Poles who managed best in Cuba were Jewish peddlers: cp. Lepkowski (1983) on Polish Jews in Mexico.
11. Mörner (1960, p. 266).
12. Bourdé (1974, p. 201; Franceschini (1908, pp. 97–98).
13. Price (1952, pp. 54–55).
14. Hernández García (1976).

15. Scobie (1964, pp. 29–30, 56–57); Cortés Conde (1968, pp. 68–69).
16. Hall (1974, pp. 179–80). On the composition of Spanish emigration, see Oddone (1966a, pp. 46–48).
17. Mulhall (1899, p. 246).
18. See Stang (1976); Stols (1976); Smolana (1983, pp. 106f., 112–16). The Polish engineers often received their training in France. Concerning the physicians in Paraguay, see Schmitt (1963, p. 79).
19. Blancpain (1974, pp. 197–200, 304–15); Roche (1959, pp. 128–32).
20. Gori (1964, pp. 90–91).
21. Cuccorese (1969, pp. 10, 18).
22. Liebermann (1966, pp. 254–55). For a recent attempt at a balanced evaluation, see Avni (1983).
23. Bourdé (1974, pp. 208–12, 228–34); Vázquez Presedo (1971, p. 609).
24. Barros Basto (1970); Nogueira (1973); Pilatti Balhana et al. (1969).
25. Vázquez (1970, pp. 87–89); Franceschini (1908, pp. 791–95). See also Worrall (1972).
26. Rodríguez Plata (1968).
27. Mosk (1955, pp. 6–20); Bergad (1980).
28. Impressions *in situ* by Mörner; cp. Eidt (1971).
29. Best known is Thomas (1954); see also Åkerman (1975, pp. 31–33).
30. On the so-called *Heydtsches Reskript* of 1859 and its revocation, see Brunn (1972, p. 298; 1971); and Diégues Júnior (1964, pp. 46–47). France and England took similar measures in 1875–76; See also Hernández García (1976).
31. Vázquez-Presedo (1971, pp. 620–22). The graph is numbered II by mistake. The variables included are: (1) percentage of capital goods imported from Great Britain (2) total immigration as a percentage of the Argentine urban population.
32. Dean (1976, pp. 157–59); Buarque de Holanda (1963, 2:294); Graham (1968, p. 101).
33. Franceschini (1908, pp. 471–73, 514–16). On a municipal level, the development is reflected in Dean (1976, p. 160, table 6.1). On the Spanish measure, see Dean (1960, p. 184). Concerning Argentina, see Solberg (1970, p. 14).
34. Sánchez-Albornoz (1974, p. 158, graph); Franceschini (1908, p. 473).
35. According to Hall (1974, p. 179). "Mass immigration in Brazil was largely the result of a boom in world coffee prices that began in the late 1880s and continued for a decade."
36. Bastos de Avila (1954, pp. 50, 90–91); see also Hall (1974, p. 179).
37. Sánchez-Albornoz (1974, p. 154).
38. Sánchez-Albornoz (1974, p. 157).

Chapter 5. The Process of Assimilation: Failures and Successes

1. Kenny (1973).
2. Solbert (1970, p. 14).

3. Mosk (1948, p. 73). On reemigration, compare Åkerman (1975, pp. 19–21).
4. Dean (1976, p. 190).
5. Kula (1976).
6. See Figure 9. Míšek (1967).
7. Hall (1974, pp. 189–91); Szuchman (1980).
8. Klein (1981). When analyzing arrest rates in Buenos Aires in 1910 by nationality, Blackwelder and Johnson (1982) found that the "much-maligned Italians" had about the same rate of lawbreaking as native Argentines, "despite ethnic discrimination and economic exploitation," while those of the Spanish were much higher. One has to note, however, that as compared to the Italians, most Spaniards in Buenos Aires at the time were newcomers who held more poorly paid and less stable jobs. The relationship between occupational status and arrest by the police was stronger than between occupation and nationality.
9. Dahl (1973); Sánchez-Albornoz (1974, p. 162).
10. Kula (1976); Smolana (1983, p. 116f.); see also Ianni (1966); Wachowicz (1976). In the case of Hungary, another poor European country, emigration to Latin America between the world wars comprsed both middle-class and poor peasant elements, according to Varga (1976).
11. Humphreys (1946, p. 65); Emílio Willems (1958; see also 1946); Roche (1959); Brunn (1971); Rios (1958); Blancpain (1974); Young (1974). The Poles and Italians in southern Brazil were also assimilated to a considerable degree once their native culture had suffered profound changes in the new country.
12. Newton (1977).
13. Platt (1964, 1965); Ferns (1960, pp. 366–67).
14. Abou (1972, pp. 363–64). On Syrio-Lebanese in Mexico, see Maloof (1959, esp. ch. 3).
15. A standard work is Saito (1961). See also Hastings (1969); Tigner (1961, 1963). Though raised in an archipelago far away from Japan (in the strict sense), the Ryukyuans remained Japanese citizens, despite U.S. occupation from 1945 until the early 1970s.
16. Worrall (1972, pp. 178–79); see also Diégues Júnior (1964, pp. 237–38).
17. For lists of such periodicals, see, for example, Roche (1959, pp. 673–74); Blancpain (1974, pp. 1039–46).
18. The main study of this topic is Solberg (1970); see also Scobie (1974, ch. 6); Cumberland (1960); Lewin, (1971, p. 171).
19. Solberg (1970); with respect to Brazil, see, for example, Marcílio (1965).
20. Hahner (1976); Quintas (1976, pp. 21–26).

Chapter 6. The Impact on the Host Countries

1. Sánchez-Albornoz (1974, p. 164).
2. Hall (1974, p. 176). For a closer examination of the Brazilian data, see Centre nationale de recherches scientifiques (1973).

3. Mörner (1960, p. 269).
4. Delhaes-Guenther (1976).
5. Bourdé (1974, pp. 192–93).
6. Solari (1958, p. 90f.) The reactions to the "melting pot" concept as applied to Latin America are represented by Bailey (1980) and Szuchman (1977).
7. Worrall (1972, p. 59).
8. Germani (1968, pp. 248, 260); see also Stang (1983) on British firms; for a detailed analysis of Italian entrepreneurs, see Scarzanella (1981).
9. Bailey (1969–70, p. 131).
10. Solberg (1970, pp. 36, 51, 54).
11. Hoetink (1970, p. 104).
12. González Loscertales (1979, 1983); Cerutti (1983); Síndico (1983); Lepkowski (1983). After 1910, the Mexican revolution fomented a massive exodus of Mexicans towards the United States. The U.S. Census of 1930 revealed that the Mexican population in the United States grew from 367,510 in 1910 to 700,541 in 1920, not including "illegals" or "whites." Between 1900 and 1930, more than a million arrived. See García (1981, pp. 35–36).
13. See, for instance, Sbarra (1955) and Gori (1952); Jacob (1969), who sees the introduction of barbed wire in Uruguay as having largely negative consequences.
14. Cortés Conde (1968, p. 88); Mosk (1948, p. 69).
15. Andrews (1980, pp. 180–88).
16. Florestan Fernandes (1970); see also other works of this famous Paulista sociologist.
17. Hall (1974, p. 192).
18. Solberg (1970, ch. 5); Lindahl (1962, pp. 272–73).
19. Solberg (1970, p. 42); Scobie (1974, pp. 237–39).
20. See, for example, Bray (1962, p. 562).
21. Cornblit (1967, pp. 211–48); Scobie (1974, pp. 212–13); Safford (1972, pp. 230–49).
22. Bagú (1969, pp. 61–62); observation by Harold Sims regarding the Japanese case.
23. Waibel (1957); Griffith (1965, pp. 301–02); Bergad (1980).
24. For Brazil, see Maram (1977), and Hall (1974).
25. Bailey (1980); however, Bailey's article does not present a methodologically satisfactory comparison; see Mörner, Fawaz de Viñuela, and French (1982, p. 65). On immigrants in unions, see also, for example, Simon (1946); Spalding (1977).
26. Hall (1974, pp. 181–82).
27. Graham (1968, pp. 137–38); Stols (1976). Stols's survey of Belgian "expansion" in Latin America toward 1900 interestingly presents all the various aspects of that impact. He sees the Belgian presence as a "security valve" for all the latent tensions and frustrated dynamics of Belgian society and also as a preparatory experience for the later Congo adventure (Stols, 1976, p. 126).
28. Vázquez-Presedo (1971, p. 624); Cortés Conde (1968, p. 73).
29. Dean (1974, pp. 231–37); Solberg (1970, pp. 50–51); L. Cafagna, quoted in Cipolla (1973, 1:303).

30. In his attempt at comparison between mass immigration in the plains of Argentina and Canada from 1870 to 1930, Solberg (1982, p. 157) concludes: "Indeed, immigration did not fundamentally change the prevailing social or political systems in either the pampas or the prairies."

Chapter 7. Immigration since 1930

1. Thistlethwaite (1960).
2. Based on López (1937).
3. Cornblit (1967, pp. 230–32).
4. López (1937).
5. López (1937).
6. See Comissão de Recenseamento da Colônia Japonesa (1964).
7. See Oddone (1966b).
8. See Elkin (1980, p. 79, table 2; p. 86).
9. Kätsch and Kätsch (1970, pp. 169, 295–97). On the Dominican Republic, see Galíndez (1956, pp. 381–85); on the Germans in Buenos Aires, see Newton (1982), who stresses that their assimilation was speeded up after the second World War. On the Jews, see Elkin (1979), esp. pp. 56, 78f. Ten thousand Jews are also estimated to have entered Argentina illegally during the 1930s and 1940s, and their situation was legalized in many cases by 1950 (Elkin, 1980, pp. 78–80).
10. Smith (1955, p. 305f.); Fagan (1973).
11. Galíndez (1956, pp. 382–85).
12. *Bevölkerung und Raum* (1965, p. 190); *Statistical Abstract of Latin America* (1967, p. 69).
13. On the Belgian refugees, see Barros Basto (1970, pp. 18, 31). On the Indochinese, UN (1982a), pp. 18, 98.
14. Nadal (1973, pp. 215–17).
15. Sims (1972); see also Hastings (1969). While persons of Japanese descent constituted just 2.5 percent of São Paulo's population, they are estimated to have controlled no less than 70 percent of both retail and wholesale trade at the Municipal Market (Tigner, 1982, p. 513). Roughly 28,000 Japanese went to Peru between 1898 and 1936 (some of whom were deported to the United States during World War II). See Gardiner (1975).
16. Sánchez-Albornoz (1974, p. 221); Diégues Júnior (1964, pp. 302–11, 338–41); Serrão (1974, p. 48, graph).
17. Suárez (1975, pp. 13–15).
18. Suárez (1975, pp. 16–17); Sánchez-Albornoz (1974, pp. 222–23); Marrero (1964, pp. 232–33). For more detail, see Kritz (1975); Sassen-Koob (1979); Chen, Urquijo, and Picquet (1982). Incredibly, there seem to be no reliable statistics for overseas immigration in Venezuela after 1974. According to international expertise, statistics on international migration to Latin America deteriorated in some cases in recent times when the importance of the phenomenon decreased (UN,

1979, p. 41). On illegal Spanish and Portuguese immigration, see ibid., p. 79.

19. Torrado (1979, pp. 432–34); Kritz and Gurak (1979, p. 410) mention 21,000 for the period 1966–77.

20. Arango Cano (1953, p. 30). Various aspects of more recent international migration in Latin America and the Caribbean are delt with in special issues of the *International Migration Review* 13; nos. 2,3 (1979). The quantitative dimension is treated in Morales Vergara (1969).

21. On the recent immigration policy of the Latin American countries, see UN (1982a, pp. 8–11). "Selective immigration" does not only comprise skilled personnel and professionals, for example. For clearly economic reasons, Mexico and Costa Rica seek to attract retired U.S. citizens and Europeans for permanent residence.

Chapter 8. Migration from and within Latin America

1. Sánchez-Albornoz (1974, p. 225); see also Meyer (1975); Bustamante (1975). Corwin (1972, pp. 188–220), underlines the lack of interest shown by historians in this topic until recently. Early migration is covered by Cardoso (1980) and Linda Hall (1982). Moore (1970) and Servín (1970) have edited useful anthologies. Notable monographs include Craig (1971); Samora (1971); Reisler (1976); and Romo (1983) on Los Angeles Chicanos. For the Oregon interviews, see Cuthbert and Stevens (1981). Estimates on the numbers of illegal Mexican immigrants in the United States vary widely. A Mexican government study in 1977–79 claimed there were "only" between a half million and a million and that most only crossed the border intending to return to Mexico within a few months. United States estimates are of four to six million (UN, 1982a, p. 74). Return migration from the United States is always hard to trace because no statistics are kept on emigration (UN, 1979, p. 43). A United Nations study group suggests that the links of the Mexican poor to the United States may be stronger than those to Mexican cities "since rural-to-urban migration within Mexico did not gain momentum until well after migration from Mexico to the South-western United States had become firmly institutionalized" (UN, 1982a, p. 64).

2. Reichert and Massey (1979, 1980).

3. Ugalde, Bean, and Cárdenas (1979); González (1979); Chaney (1979, p. 204). Of all the documented migrants entering the United States in 1975–76, 40 percent were from Latin America and the Caribbean. Fifteen percent were Mexicans—to whom all the illegal immigrants should be added! In Canada, in 1977, the Latin American–Caribbean share was 18 percent (UN, 1982a, p. 3).

4. Sánchez-Albornoz (1974, p. 225f.); Matterlart and Matterlart (1964, p. 157). For a bibliography on the subject, see Cordasco, Buccioni, and Castellanos (1972), which lists 754 titles. Since 1971, reemigration has exceeded immigration (UN 1979, p. 43).

5. Williams-Bailey and Pemberton (1972, pp. 156–59); Roberts (1963, pp. 104–06).

6. Anselm (1979, p. 37).

7. MacGaffey and Barnett (1962, pp. 36, 42–43); Fagen, Brody, and O'Leary (1968); Valdés and Lieuwen (1971, pp. 96–99); Rogg (1974).

8. UN (1982a, pp. 97, 99); ECLA (1980, p. 183). Our information is also based on testimony presented to the U.S. Senate by church officals from Miami.

9. Lundahl (1979, pp. 623–28); Laquerre (1983); UN (1982a, p. 73).

10. According to the Intergovernmental Committee for European Migration (ICEM). Statistics kindly provided by the Swedish section of Amnesty International.

11. Sánchez-Albornoz (1974, p. 226f.). Rockett (1976) does not believe that the flow increased during the early 1970s. Torrado (1979, p. 435) estimates the Latin American exodus of professionals and technicians, 1969–70, at 61,000 persons. See also Oteiza (1971).

12. Palmer (1983) finds that the emigration of 230,000 Jamaicans to the United States and Canada, 1967–78, had a clearly detrimental effect on Jamaica's development due to the high precentage of white-collar and skilled workers. Emigrants in 1978 alone constituted no less than 4.5 percent of the island's resources of active professionals and technicans.

13. Weisbrot (1980, pp. 95–101) reckons that there are a half million Jews in Argentina, but Elkin's careful estimate reduces that total to 286,000 (1979, p. 193f.).

14. UN (1982a, pp. 1, 62–64, 72–76). Between Mexico and the United States the wage differential has normally been seven to one, in some cases even thirteen to one.

15. See Bauer (1975, p. 152f.).

16. Roberts (1963, p. 107); Dahl (1960). For Jamaicans in Costa Rica, see Casey (1978).

17. Lundahl (1982); Pérez de la Riva (1975).

18. Galíndez (1956, pp. 337–80); UN (1982a, p. 57).

19. Sassen-Koob (1979). Admittedly there is also a current of skilled or professional Colombians who simply overstay their visa or tourist permits to take better-paid jobs in Venezuela (UN, 1982a, p. 75).

20. Sánchez-Albornoz (1974, p. 238). See also A. Vieytes (1982) and UN (1982a, p. 73). El Salvador is one of the very few Latin American nations that recognizes the need for emigration. The government has tried to organize labor export to Bolivia and Saudi Arabia (UN, 1982a, p. 17).

21. Sánchez-Albornoz (1974, p. 239); Carrón (1979); Morales (1974). According to Marshall and Orlansky (1983), labor demand and push factors, not changes in immigration policy, determined the rhythm of Argentine immigration.

22. Gillespie and Browning (1979); Petrucelli (1979). At the same time, internal migration in Uruguay decreased between 1963 and 1975, due to the overall economic stagnation, as Viega (1981) points out. As observed by Butterworth and Chance (1981, p. 81), the "effects of out-migration and return migration on

communities of origin have probably received the least attention of any aspect of internal migration." Yet the early article by González (1961), for instance, makes important distinctions between the various types of migrant wage labor in this regard. The extreme poverty of Haiti is relieved by the remittances of the migrants which contribute about 5 percent of Haiti's GNP (UN 1982a, p. 74). Estimates with respect to remittances by Mexicans in the United States differ widely, from the Mexican estimate of 300 million to the U.S. estimate of two billion dollars (UN, 1982a, p. 65).

23. On colonization in the tropics, see, for example, Crist (1964); Brisseau (1970) and several essays in *Les phénomènes de frontière dans les pays tropicaux* (1981). Venezuelan Guyana had 51,000 inhabitants in 1971, 87 percent of whom had arrived since 1961 (Chen, 1978, p. 81). The Amazon scheme is best analysed by Kohlhepp (1976, 1980).

24. Sánchez-Albornoz (1974, pp. 23–38); Duncan and Rutledge (1977, pp. 203–67) includes articles by Rutledge, Klarén and Favre. See also Blanchard (1979).

25. See Mörner (1978, pp. 7–29). For an analysis of several waves of Indian migrants in the South Peruvian city of Arequipa, 1575–1615, see Sánchez-Albornoz (1982a); see also his article on the role of migration in Upper Peru during the mid-seventeenth century (1982b).

26. Poppino (1968), pp. 141, 146; Hirschman (1965, ch. 1); Hirschman's interpretation was partly challenged by Lindqvist (1973, pp. 32–112).

27. Cook (1970); Borah and Cook (1976); Les migrations au Mexique (1975). See also Butterworth and Chance (1978, pp. 15–18).

28. Castellano de Sjöstrand (1975). In Mexico, during recent years, a similar rush to the oil fields has taken place.

29. IDB (1981), p. 395.

30. *Statistical Abstract of Latin America* (1980, p. 77). For earlier times, see Sánchez-Albornoz (1974, pp. 242–47); Morse (1971), and Elízaga (1972).

31. Sánchez-Albornoz (1974, pp. 248–50).

32. Morse (1971, no. 1, pp. 19–20); Elízaga (1972, p. 141). For an especially lucid discussion of rural-to-urban migration see Odell and Preston (1978, pp. 109–21).

33. Gino Germani, quoted in Morse (1971, no. 1, p. 14).

34. Wilkie (1970).

35. This is one of the conclusions of the exceptionally detailed study of Elízaga (1970). It is a monograph of migration in Chile based on interviews with some 11,000 people. On the other hand, unemployment runs as a real thread through the study of Niño de Guerrero (1975).

36. Elízaga (1972, p. 141).

37. Morse (1971, no. 1, pp. 23–24); this point is underlined by, among others, McGreevey (1968). See also Butterworth and Chance (1981, pp. 81–90, 131–35).

38. Morse (1971, no. 1, pp. 22–23); Elízaga (1972, pp. 142–43).

39. One of the very few studies on the subject is Feindt and Browning (1972), which deals with Monterrey. See also Simmons and Cardona (1972); Preston, Taveras, and Preston (1981).

40. Eduardo E. Arriaga, quoted in Morse (1971, no. 1, p. 17; see also p. 18).
41. Germani (1968, pp. 306–07).
42. Sánchez-Albornoz (1974, pp. 250–51).
43. However, the notion of "tertiarization," that is, an abnormal growth of the tertiary sector, is criticized by Morse (1971, no. 2, pp. 19–24).
44. Butterworth and Chance (1981, pp. 151–57), with references to literature.
45. Butterworth and Chance (1981, pp. 160–67).
46. The analysis is based upon population figures for Havana derived from the censuses and official estimates of 1943, 1961, 1970 and 1978. The calculations of average annual rates made by Harold Sims utilize the earliest year as base (the rate for the period was simply divided by the number of years). Nicaragua was included in the generalization because the new revolutionary regime is pursuing Cuban-style policies, encouraging rural and frontier settlement, building rural schools and extending health and social services to the countryside. Since the revolution there is proceeding at an escalated pace, Nicaragua may abbreviate or miss entirely the Cuban pattern of urban growth in the first decade. These conclusions were reached by Sims after a tour of the country in 1980 during which he interviewed development officials and observed the literacy campaign.

Final Remarks

1. Butterworth and Chance (1981, p. 35), commenting on Mangalam and Schwartzweller (1969).
2. Based on Wood (1982). See also Bach and Schraml (1982) and Nikolinakos's short presentation of the historical-structural view (1975) and the critical review of his arguments by Shanin (1978).
3. Wolf (1982, p. 362f.).
4. Germani (1968) saw immigration as a means of bringing about an Argentine "modernization," that vague, elusive concept.
5. Hall (1974, p. 192).
6. Wolf (1982, pp. 379–81). Even the many years of the Castro regime do not seem to have resolved the race problem entirely. The present turmoil in "revolutionary" Suriname should also be noticed.
7. According to Butterworth and Chance (1981), "Migration is often a major symptom of basic social change." A recent United Nations document also makes clear that the trend toward curbing undocumented or illegal immigration from the Third world in the developed countries can be seen as "another symptom of persistent inequalities in the prevailing international economic order" (UN, 1982a, p. 81).
8. According to a United Nations estimate, Mexico City, by the year 2000 the world's largest agglomeration, will have 31 million inhabitants; São Paulo, next in order, will have 26 million; Rio de Janeiro (number 7) will have 19 million; Buenos Aires (number 15) will have 12 million people. "Megacity" is a concept

coined for agglomerations of 10 million or more inhabitants (see UN, 1982b, pp. 154, 158). See also Preston and Odell (1978, p. 109) and Rogers (1982, p. 487), who takes a rather sanguine view of these frightening prospects.

9. Bach and Schraml (1982, p. 326f.). "Refugees have accounted for more than half of all international migration since the end of the First World War and constitute an increasing share of current flows," claims a group of international experts, with reference to the global situation (UN, 1982a, p. 84). Refugees are more numerous now than at any time since the end of World War II. Yet the numbers in Latin America are small—quite small if compared to the situation in Africa and Asia.

Bibliography

Abou, Selim. 1972. *Immigrés dans l'autre Amérique: Autobiographies de quatre Argentins d'origine libanaise*. Paris: Plon.

Adamson, Alan H. 1972. *Sugar without slaves: The political economy of British Guiana, 1838–1904*. New Haven, Conn.: Yale University Press.

Åkerman, Sune. 1975. *From Stockholm to San Francisco: The development of the historical study of external migrations*. Uppsala: Commission Internationale d'Historie des Mouvements Sociaux et des Structures Sociales.

Alden, Dauril, and Warren Dean, eds. 1977. *Essays concerning the socioeconomic history of Brazil and Portugal*. Gainesville: University Presses of Florida.

Alsina, Juan A. 1910. *La inmigración en el primer siglo de la independencia*. Buenos Aires: F.S. Alsina.

Anderle, A. 1976. La emigración húngara a la América Latina después de la derrota de la revolución de 1848–49. *Jahrbuch für Geschichte von Staat, Wirtschaft und Gesellschaft Lateinamerikas* 13:56–83.

Andrews, George Reid. 1980. *The Afro-Argentines of Buenos Aires, 1800–1900*. Madison: University of Wisconsin Press.

Ankum-Houwink, J. 1974. Chinese contract migrants in Surinam between 1853 and 1870. *Boletín de Estudios Latinoamericanos y del Caribe* (The Hague) 17:42–68.

Anselm, Alain. 1979. *L'emigration antillaise en France: Du Bantoustan au ghetto*. Paris: Editions Anthropos.

Antonione, A. 1965. El padrón de Montevideo de 1743. *América colonial: Población y economía. Anuario* (Rosario, Argentina): 113–18.

Arango Cano, Jesús. 1953. *Inmigración y colonización en la Gran Colombia*. Bogotá: Librería Voluntad.

Argentina, Republic of. Dirección de Inmigración. 1925. *Resumen estadístico del movimiento migratorio en la República Argentina, 1857–1924*. Buenos Aires.

Arquivo Nacional. 1960. *Registro de estrangeiros, 1808–1822*. Rio de Janeiro.

———. 1963. *Registro de estrangeiros nas capitanias, 1777–1819*. Rio de Janeiro.

Audera, Víctor. 1955. *La población y la inmigración en Hispanoamérica.* Madrid: Ediciones Cultura Hispánica.

Avila, Fernando Bastos de. 1954. *Economic impact of immigration: The Brazilian immigration problem.* The Hague: Nijhoff.

———. 1964. *Immigration in Latin America.* Washington, D.C.: Pan American Union. Secretariat General of the Organization of American States.

Avni, Haim. 1983. La agricultura judía en la Argentina: Éxito o fracaso? *Desarrollo Económico* 22 (no. 88): 535–48.

Bach, Robert L., and Lisa A. Schraml. 1982. Migration, crisis and theoretical conflict. *International Migration Review* 16 (no. 2): 320–41.

Badura, Bohumil. 1971. Los franceses en Santiago de Cuba a mediados del año de 1808. *Ibero-Americana Pragensia* (Prague) 5:157–60.

———. 1975. Sobre la inmigración alemana en Cuba durante la primera mitad del siglo XIX. *Ibero-Americana Pragensia* (Prague) 9:79–80.

Bagú, Sergio. 1966. *El plan económico del grupo rivadaviano, 1811–1827.* Rosario, Argentina: Instituto de Investigaciones Históricas.

———. 1969. *Evolución histórica de la estratificación social en la Argentina.* Caracas: Esquema.

Baily, Samuel L. 1967. The Italians and organized labor in the United States and Argentina: 1880–1910. *International Migration Review* 1:55–66.

———. 1977. Patterns of assimilation of Italians in Buenos Aires, 1880–1940. Presented at the annual meeting of the American Historical Association, Dallas.

———. 1978. The role of the press and the assimilation of Italians in Buenos Aires and São Paulo. *International Migration Review* 12:321–40.

———. 1979. Italians in Buenos Aires, 1880–1940: An approach to the study of cultural pluralism, Presented at the annual meeting of the Organization of American Historians, New Orleans.

———. 1980. Marriage patterns and immigration assimilation in Buenos Aires, 1883–1923. *Hispanic American Historical Review* 60 (no. 7): 32–48.

Bairoch, Paul. 1965. Niveaux de développement économique de 1810 à 1910. *Annales E.-S.-C.* (Paris) 20 (no. 6): 1091–1117.

Barros Basto, Fernando Lázaro de. 1970. *Síntese da historia da inmigracão no Brasil.* Rio de Janeiro: n.p.

Bates, Margaret. 1957. *The migration of peoples to Latin America.* Washington, D.C.: Catholic University of America Press.

Bauer, Arnold J. 1975. *Chilean rural society from the Spanish conquest to 1930.* Cambridge: Cambridge University Press.

Bennassar, Bartolomé. 1976. La inmigración francesa a la Argentina a finales del siglo XIX: El caso de la colonia de Pigüe y el problema de las fuentes. *Jahrbuch für Geschichte von Staat, Wirtschaft und Gesellschaft Lateinamerikas* 13:174–80.

———. 1977. *Les Aveyronnais dans la pampa: Fondation, développement et vie de la colonie aveyronnaise de Pigüe, Argentina, 1884–1974.* Toulouse: Privat.

Bergad, Laird W. 1980. Puerto Rico, Puerto pobre: Coffee and the growth of agrarian capitalism in nineteenth-century Puerto Rico. Ph.D. diss., University of Pittsburgh.

Berglund-Thompson, Susan Anne. 1980. *The "Musiues" in Venezuela: Immigration goals and reality, 1936–1961.* Ph.D. diss., University of Massachusetts, Amherst.

Bernhard, Virginia, ed. 1979. *Elites, masses, and modernization in Latin America, 1850–1940.* Austin: University of Texas Press.

Berninger, Dieter Georg. 1974. *La inmigración en México (1821–1857).* Mexico City: Sepsetentas.

Bevölkerung und Raum in der Weltgeschichte. 1965. 3d ed. Würzburg, West Germany: Ploetz.

Blakemore, Harold. 1979. La emigración británica a América Latina: Algunas observaciones generales sobre el tema, las fuentes y la investigación. In *La emigración europea a la América Latina: Fuentes y estado de investigación: Informes presentados a la IVᵃ Reunión de Historiadores Latinoamericanistas Europeos.* West Berlin: Colloquium Verlag.

Blanchard, Peter. 1979. The recruitment of workers in the Peruvian Sierra at the turn of the century: The enganche system. *Inter-American Economic Affairs* 33 (no. 3): 3:63–83.

Blackwelder, Julia Kirk, and Lyman L. Johnson. 1982. Changing criminal patterns in Buenos Aires, 1890 to 1914. *Journal of Latin American Studies* 14:359–80.

Blancpain, Jean Pierre. 1974. *Les allemands au Chili (1816–1945).* Cologne: Böhlau.

Bobińska, Celina, and Adam Galos. 1975. Poland: Land of mass emigration (19th and 20th centuries). *Poland at the 14th International Congress of Historical Sciences in San Francisco.* Wroclaw: Polish Academy of Sciences: 172–75.

Bobińska, Celina, and A. Pilch, eds. 1975. *Employment-seeking emigrations of the Poles world-wide: XIX and XX centuries.* Krakow: Jagiellanskiego.

Borah, Woodraw, and S. F. Cook. 1976. The urban center as a focus of migration in the colonial period: New Spain (17th and 18th century in Latin America). In *Atti del XL: Congrèsso Internazionale degli Americanisti, Roma, Genova, 3–10 settembre 1972* (Genoa) 4:158–67.

Borges Morán, Pedro. 1977. *El envío de misioneros a América durante la época española.* Salamanca: Universidad pontificia.

Bourdé, Guy. 1974. *Urbanisation et immigration en Amérique Latine: Buenos Aires XIXᵉ et XXᵉ siècles.* Paris: Aubier.

Boyd-Bowman, Peter. 1964. *Indice geográfico de 40,000 pobladores de América en el siglo XVI.* Vol. 1, *La etapa antillana, 1493–1519.* Bogotá: Instituto Caro y Cuervo.

―――. 1968. *Indice geográfico de 40,000 pobladores de América en el siglo XVI.* Vol. 2, *1520–1539.* Mexico City: Editorial Jus.

―――. 1973. *Patterns of Spanish emigration to the New World (1493–1580).* Buffalo: State University of New York.

―――. 1976ᵃ. Spanish emigrants to the Indies, 1595–98: A profile. In *First images*

of America: The impact of the New World on the Old. Ed. Fredi Chiappelli.
Berkeley: University of California Press.

———. 1976b. Patterns of Spanish emigration to the Indies until 1600. *Hispanic American Historical Review* 66 (no. 4):580–604.

———. 1976/1977. Patterns of Spanish emigration to the Indies, 1579–1600. *The Americas* 33 (no. 1):78–95.

Brading, David A. 1973. Los españoles en México hacia 1792. *Historia Mexicana* 23 (no. 1):126–44.

Bray, Donald W. 1962. The political emergence of Arab Chileans, 1952–58. *Journal of Inter-American Studies* 4:557–62.

Brisseau, Jeanine. 1970. Le rôle du Cuzco dans la colonisation de la "ceja de montaña" y de la "montaña." In *Villes et régions en Amérique Latine.* Paris: Institut des Hautes Etudes de l'Amérique Latine.

Bromley, Rosemary D. F., and Ray Bromley. 1982. *South American development: A geographical introduction.* Cambridge: Cambridge University Press.

Brown, Jonathan. 1979. *A socio-economic history of Argentina.* Cambridge: Cambridge University Press.

Brunn, Gerhard. 1971. *Deutschland und Brasilien (1889–1914).* Cologne: Böhlau.

———. 1972. Die Bedeutung von Einwanderung und Kolonisation im brasilianischen Kaiserreich (1818–1889). *Jahrbuch für Geschichte von Staat, Wirtschaft und Gesellschaft Lateinamerikas* 9:292–98.

Buarque de Holanda, Sérgio, ed. 1963. *História geral da civilização brasileira: O Brasil monarquico.* 2 vols. 2d ed. São Paulo: Difusão Européia do Livro.

Burkett, Elinor C. 1975. Early colonial Peru: The urban female experience. Ph.D. diss., University of Pittsburgh.

Calafut, George. 1977. Analysis of Italian immigration statistics, 1876–1914. *Jahrbuch für Geschichte von Staat, Wirtschaft und Gesellschaft Lateinamerikas* 14:310–30.

The Cambridge economic history of Europe. Ed. M. Postan and J. Habakkuk. 1965. Vol. 6, *Industrial revolution and after.* Cambridge: Cambridge University Press.

Campbell, Leon G. 1972. The foreigners in Peruvian society during the eighteenth century. *Revista de Historia de América* (Mexico City) 73/74:153–63.

Cándido, S. 1976. La emigración política italiana a la América Latina (1820–1870). *Jahrbuch für Geschichte von Staat, Wirtschaft und Gesellschaft Lateinamerikas* 13:56–83.

Capitales, empresarios y obreros europeos en América Latina: Actas del 6º Congreso de AHILA, Estocolmo, 25–28 de mayo de 1981. 1983. 2 vols. Stockholm: Instituto de Estudios Latinoamericanos.

Carande, Ramón. 1943. *Carlos V y sus banqueros.* 2 vols. Madrid: Revista de Occidente.

Cardona, R., et al. 1980. *El éxodo de Colombianos: Un estudio de la corriente migratoria a los Estados Unidos y un intento para propiciar el retorno.* Bogotá: Ediciones Tercer Mundo.

Cardoso, Lawrence A. 1980. *Mexican emigration to the United States, 1897–1931: Socioeconomic patterns.* Tucson: University of Arizona Press.

Cardozo, Manoel. 1946. The Brazilian gold rush. *The Americas* 3(no. 2):137–60.

Carmagnani, Marcello, and Giovanna Mantelli. 1979. Fuentes cuantitativas italianas relativas a la emigración italiana: Un análisis crítico. In *La emigración europea a la América Latina: Fuentes y estado de investigación.* West Berlin: Colloquium Verlag.

Carrón, Juan M. 1979a. Migraciones interregionales en América Latina. *Revista Paraguaya de Sociología* 16 (no. 46):7–24.

―――. 1979b. Shifting patterns in migration from bordering countries to Argentina: 1914–1970. *International Migration Review* 13:475–87.

Casey, Jeffrey J. 1975. La inmigración china. *Revista de Historia* (Heredia, Costa Rica) 1 (no. 1):145–65.

―――. 1978. La industria bananera en Costa Rica (1800–1940): La organización social del trabajo. *Revista de Indias* 38 (nos. 153/54):739–89.

Centre nationale de Recherches scientifiques. 1973. *L'histoire quantitative du Brésil de 1800 à 1930: Coloques internationales de CNRS, 11–15 Oct. 1971.* Paris: IHEAL.

Cerutti, Mario. 1983. La formación de capitales preindustriales en Monterrey (1850–1890): Inmigrantes y configuración de una burguesía regional. *Capitales* 2.

Chaney, Elsa M. 1979. The world economy and contemporary migration. *International Migration Review* 13 (no. 2): 202–12.

Chaunu, Pierre, and Huguette Chaunu. 1955–1958. *Séville et l'Atlantique, 1504–1650.* 8 vols. Paris: SEVPEN.

Chen, Chi-Yen. 1978. *Desarrollo regional-urbano y ordenamiento del territorio: Mito y realidad.* Caracas: Universidad Católica Andrés Bello.

Chen, Chi-Yen, José I. Urquijo, and Michel Picquet. 1982. Los movimientos migratorios internacionales en Venezuela: Políticas y realidades. *Revista de investigaciones sobre relaciones industriales y laborales* (Caracas) 4 (nos. 10/11): 11–47.

Chuaqui, Benedicto. 1942. *Memorias de un emigrante (imágenes y confidencias).* Santiago de Chile: Ediciones Orbe.

Cipolla, Carlo M., ed. 1973. *The Fontana economic history of Europe: The emergence of industrial societies.* Vols. 1, 2. London: Collins.

Comissão de Recenseamento da Colônia Japonesa, São Paulo, Brazil. 1964. *The Japanese immigrant in Brazil: Statistical tables.* Tokyo: University of Tokyo Press.

Conrad, Robert. 1975. The planter class and the debate over Chinese immigration to Brazil, 1850–1893. *International Migration Review* 9 (no. 1):41–55.

Consejo Latinoamericano de Ciencias Sociales. 1973. *Migración y desarrollo 2: Consideraciones teóricas y aspectos socioeconómicos y políticos.* Buenos Aires: CLACSO.

―――. 1974a. *Migración y desarrollo 1: Consideraciones teóricas.* Buenos Aires: Nueva Visión.

―――. 1974b. *Migración y desarrollo 3: Análisis históricos y aspectos relacionados a la estructura agraria y al proceso de urbanización.* Buenos Aires: CLACSO.

————. n.d. *Migración y desarrollo 4: Las relaciones campo-ciudad a través del proceso migratorio*. Buenos Aires: CLACSO.

————. 1976. *Las migraciones internas en América Latina: Bibliografía*. Asunción: Centro Paraguayo de Estudios Sociólogos, Centro Paraguayo de Documentación Social.

Consejo Superior de Investigaciones Científicas. 1940–1946. *Catálogo de pasajeros a India durante los siglos XVI, XVII y XVIII*. Vol. 1, *1509–1534*. Vol. 2, *1535–1538*. Vol. 3, *1539–1559*. Seville: Consejo Superior de Investigaciones Científicas.

Cook, Sherburne F. 1970. Las migraciones en la historia de la población mexicana: Datos modelo del occidente del centro de México, 1793–1950. In *Historia y sociedad en el mundo de habla española: Homenaje a José Miranda*. Ed. Bernardo García Martínez et al. Mexico City: El Colegio de México.

Corbett, T. G. 1974. Migration to a Spanish imperial frontier in the seventeenth and eighteenth centuries: St. Augustine. *Hispanic American Historical Review* 54:414–30.

Corbitt, Duvon Clough. 1942. Immigration in Cuba. *Hispanic American Historical Review* 22:280–308.

————. 1971. *A study of the Chinese in Cuba, 1847–1947*. Wilmore, Ky.: Asbury College, 1971.

Cordasco, Francesco, E. Buccioni, and D. Castellanos. 1972. *Puerto Ricans on the United States mainland: A bibliography of reports, texts, critical studies and related materials*. Totowa, N.J.: Rowman and Littlefield.

Cornblit, Oscar. 1967. European immigrants in Argentine industry and politics. In *The politics of conformity in Latin America*. Ed. Claudio Véliz. Oxford: Oxford University Press.

Cortés Conde, Roberto. 1968. La expansión de la economía argentina entre 1870 y 1914 y el papel de la inmigración. *Caravelle: Cahiers du monde hispanic et luso-brésilien* (Tolosa) 10:67–88.

Corwin, Arthur F. 1972. Historia de la emigración mexicana, 1900–1970: Literatura e investigacion. *Historia Mexicana* (Mexico City) 22 (no. 2):188–220.

Corwin, Arthur F., ed. 1978. *Immigrants and immigrants: Perspectives on Mexican labor migration to the U.S.* Westport, Conn.: Greenwood.

Craig, Richard B. 1971. *The bracero program*. Austin: University of Texas Press.

Crist, Raymond E. 1964. *Andean America: Some aspects of human migration and settlement*. Nashville, Tenn.: Vanderbilt University.

Cuccorese, Horacio Juan. 1969. *Historia de los ferrocarriles en la Argentina*. Buenos Aires: Macchi.

Cumberland, Charles C. 1960. The Sonora Chinese and the Mexican revolution. *Hispanic American Historical Review* 40:191–223.

Cuthbert, Richard W., and J. B. Stevens. 1981. The net economic incentives for illegal Mexican migrants: A case study. *International Migration Review* 15 (no. 3):543–50.

Dahl, Víctor C. 1960. Alien labor on the gulf coast of Mexico, 1800–1900. *The Americas* 18 (no. 1):21–35.

———. 1973. Yugoslav immigrant experiences in Argentina and Chile. *Inter-American Affairs* 28 (no. 3):3–26.

Dall'Alba, Leonir, 1971. *Pioneros nas terras dos condes: História de Orleans.* Orleans: n.p.

Davatz, Thomas. 1972. *Memórias de um colono no Brasil (1850).* São Paulo: Livraria Martins Editora.

Dean, Warren. 1974. Remessas de dinheiro dos inmigrantes italianos do Brasil, Argentina, Uruguay e Estados Unidos da América (1844–1914). *Anais de história* (São Paulo) 6:231–37.

———. 1976. *Rio Claro: A Brazilian plantation system, 1820–1920.* Stanford, Calif.: Stanford University Press.

Delhaes-Guenther, Dietrich von. 1973. Ein Jahrhundert italienische Auswanderung nach Brasilien: Betrachtungen über die Gesamtauswanderung und deren Anfängen. *Jahrbuch für Geschichte von Staat, Wirtschaft und Gesellschaft Lateinamerikas* 10:351–53.

———. 1976. La influencia de la inmigración en el desarrollo y composición de la población de Río Grande do Sul. *Jahrbuch für Geschichte von Staat, Wirtschaft und Gesellschaft Lateinamerikas* 13:420–33.

Diégues Júnior, Manuel. 1964. *Imigração e industrialização (Estudo sôbre alguns aspectos da contribuição cultural do imigrante no Brasil).* Rio de Janeiro: Centro Brasileiro de Pesquisas Educacionais.

Dore, Grazia. 1964. *La democrazia italiana e l'emigrazione in America.* Brescia: Biblioteca di storia contemporanea.

Duncan, Kenneth, and Ian Rutledge, eds. 1977. *Land and labour in Latin America: Essays on the development of agrarian capitalism in the nineteenth and twentieth centuries.* Cambridge: Cambridge University Press.

Duprey, Jacques. 1952. *Voyage aux origines françaises de l'Uruguay.* Montevideo: Instituto Histórico y Geográfico del Uruguay.

ECLA. 1982. *Statistical yearbook for Latin America.* New York: United Nations Economic Commission for Latin America.

Eidt, Robert C. 1971. *Pioneer settlements in northeast Argentina.* Madison: University of Wisconsin Press.

Elízaga, Juan C. 1970. *Migraciones a las áreas metropolitanas de América Latina.* Santiago de Chile: CELADE.

———. 1972. International migration: An overview. *International Migration Review* 6 (no. 2):121–46.

Elkin, Judith L. 1980. *Jews of the Latin American republics.* Chapel Hill: University of North Carolina Press.

La emigración europea a la América Latina: Fuentes y estado de investigación: Informes presentados a la IV^a Reunión de Historiadores Latinoamericanistas Europeos. 1979. West Berlin: Colloquium Verlag.

Engermann, Stanley L. and Eugene D. Genovese, eds. 1975. *Race and slavery in the Western Hemisphere: Quantitative studies*. Princeton, N.J.: Princeton University Press.

Estadistica de la emigración e immigración de España en el quinquenio 1896–1900. 1903.

Everaert, John. 1976. El movimiento emigratorio desde Amberes a la América Latina durante el siglo XIX (1830–1914). *Jahrbuch für Geschichte von Staat, Wirtschaft und Gesellschaft Lateinamerikas* 13:331–60.

————. 1979. Emigración desde Amberes a América Latina (1830–1914): Fuentes belgas y estado de la investigación. In *La emigración europea a la América latina: Fuentes y estado de investigación: Informes presentados a la IVᵃ Reunión de Historiadores Latinoamericanistas Europeos*. West Berlin: Colloquium Verlag.

Fagen, Patricia W. 1973. *Exiles and citizens: Spanish republicans in Mexico*. Austin, Tex.: ILAS.

Fagen, Richard R., Richard A. Brody, and Thomas J. O'Leary. 1968. *Cubans in exile: Disaffection and the revolution*. Stanford, Calif.: Stanford University Press.

Feindt, Waltraut, and Harley L. Browning. 1972. Return migration: Its significance in an industrial metropolis and an agricultural town in Mexico. *International Migration Review* 6 (no. 2):158–65.

Ferenczi, Imre, and Walter F. Willcox, eds. 1929. *International Migrations*. Vols. 1, 2. New York: National Bureau of Economic Research.

Fernandes, Florestan. 1970. Immigration and race relations in São Paulo. In *Race and class in Latin America*. Ed. Magnus Mörner. New York: Columbia University Press.

Ferns, H. S. 1960. *Britain and Argentina in the nineteenth century*. Oxford: Clarendon Press.

Foerster, Robert F. 1919. *The Italian emigration of our times*. Vol. 2. New York: Russell and Russell.

Fonseca, Luisa da. 1953. O Brasil e os estrangeiros: Mercaderes. *Proceedings of the international colloquium on Luso-Brazilian studies . . . 1950*. Nashville, Tenn.: Vanderbilt University Press.

Franceschini, Antonio. 1908. *L'emigrazione italiana nell'America del Sud*. Rome: Forzani E.C. Tipografi Editori.

Fretz, Joseph Winfield. 1953. *Pilgrims in Paraguay: The story of Mennonite colonization in South America*. Scottdale, Pa.: Herold Press.

Friede, Juan. 1952. Algunas observaciones sobre la realidad de la emigración española a América en la primera mitad del siglo XVI. *Revista de Indias* (Madrid) 13 (no. 49):467–96.

Galíndez, Jesús de. 1956. *La era de Trujillo*. Santiago de Chile: Ediciones del Pacífico.

García, Mario T. 1981. *Desert immigrants: The Mexicans of El Paso, 1880–1920*. New Haven, Conn.: Yale University Press.

García Martínez, Bernardo, et al., eds. 1970. *Historia y sociedad en el mundo de habla española: Homenaje a José Miranda*. Mexico City: El Colegio de México.

Gardiner, C. Harvey. 1975. *The Japanese and Peru, 1873–1973.* Albuquerque: University of New Mexico Press.

Germani, Gino. 1968. *Política y sociedad en una época de transición: De la sociedad tradicional a la sociedad de masas.* Buenos Aires: Paidos.

Gillespie, Francis, and Harley Browning. 1979. The effect of emigration upon socioeconomic structure: The case of Paraguay. *International Migration Review* 13 (no. 3):502–18.

Godio, Julio. 1983. Migrantes europeos y organización del movimiento obrero argentino, 1880–1900. *Capitales* 1:314–48.

Góngora, Mario. 1969. *Los grupos de conquistadores en Tierra Firme (1509–1530): Fisonomía histórico-social de un tipo de conquista.* Santiago de Chile: Universidad de Chile.

Gonzales, Nancie L. 1961. Family organization in five types of migratory wage labor. *American Anthropologist* 63 (no. 6):1264–80.

———. 1979. Garifuna settlement in New York: A new frontier. *International Migration Review* 13 (no. 2):255–63.

Gonzalez Loscertales, Vicente. 1979. Bases para el análisis socio económico de la colonia española de México en 1910. *Revista de Indias* 39 (nos. 155–58):267–95.

Gori, Gastón. 1952. *La pampa sin gaucho: Influencia del inmigrante en la transformación de los usos y costumbres en el campo argentino en el siglo XIX.* Buenos Aires: Raigal.

———. 1964. *Inmigración y colonización en la Argentina.* Buenos Aires: Eudeba.

Gouy, Patrice. 1980. *Péregrination des "Barcelonettes" au Mexique.* Grenoble: Presses Universitaires.

Graham, Richard. 1968. *Great Britain and the onset of modernization in Brazil, 1850–1914.* Cambridge: Cambridge University Press.

Graham, Richard, and Peter H. Smith, eds. 1974. *New approaches to Latin American history.* Austin: University of Texas Press.

Griffith, William J. 1965. *Empires in the wilderness: Foreign colonization and development in Guatemala, 1834–1844.* Chapel Hill: University of North Carolina Press.

Groniowski, Krzysztof. 1972. *Polska emigracja zarobkowa w Brazylii, 1871–1914.* Wroclaw: Ossolineum. (Summary in English.)

———. 1979, A emigração polonesa para a América Latina nos séculos XIX e XX. In *La emigración europea a la América Latina: Fuentes y estado de investigación: Informes presentados a la IVª Reunión de Historiadores Latinoamericanistas Europeos.* West Berlin: Colloquium Verlag.

Hack, H. n.d. *Die Kolonisation der Mennoniten im paraguayischen Chaco.* Amsterdam: K. Tropeninstitut.

Hägerstrand, Torsten. 1969. On the definition of migration. *Yearbook of Population Research in Finland.* Helsinki: Väestöpoliittinen Tutkimuslaitos.

Hahner, June E. 1976. Jacobinos versus Galegos: Urban radicals versus Portuguese immigrants in Rio de Janeiro in the 1890s. *Journal of Inter-American Studies and World Affairs* 18 (no. 2): 125–54.

Hall, Linda. 1982. El refugio: Migración mexicana a los Estados Unidos, 1910–1920. *Históricas: Boletín de información* 8:23–38.

Hall, Michael M. 1974. Approaches to immigration history. In *New approaches to Latin American history*. Ed. Richard Graham and Peter H. Smith. Austin: University of Texas Press:175–93.

Halpern Pereira, Miriam. 1982. *A política portuguesa de emigração (1850–1930)*. Lisboa: Editora A. Regra do Jogo.

Hanna, Alfred Jackson, and Katherine Abbey Hanna. 1960. *Confederate exiles in Venezuela*. Tuscaloosa, Ala. Confederate Publishing Co.

Hardoy, Jorge E., and Carmen Aranovich. 1967. Cuadro comparativo de los centros de colonización española existentes en 1580 y 1630. *Desarrollo Económico* 7 (no. 27):531–60.

———. 1970. Urban scales and function in Spanish America toward the year 1600: First conclusions. *Latin American Research Review* 5 (no. 3):57–110.

Hasbrouck, Alfred. [1928] 1969. *Foreign legionaires in the liberation of Spanish South America*. Reprint. New York: Octagon Books.

Hastings, Donald. 1969. Japanese emigration and assimilation in Brazil. *International Migration Review* 4 (no. 2):32–53.

Hernández Alvarez, José. 1967. *Return migration to Puerto Rico*. Berkeley and Los Angeles: University of California Press.

Hernández García, Julio. 1976. Algunos aspectos de la emigración de las Islas Canarias a Hispanoamérica en la segunda mitad del siglo XIX (1840–1895). *Jahrbuch für Geschichte von Staat, Wirtschaft und Gesellschaft Lateinamerikas* 13:132–50.

———. 1979. Informe sobre fuentes existentes en España para un estudio de la emigración española a Ibero-América durante el siglo XIX. In *La emigración europea a la América Latina: Fuentes y estado de investigación: Informes presentados a la IVª Reunión de Historiadores Latinoamericanistas Europeos*. West Berlin: Colloquium Verlag.

Hernández Sánchez-Barba, Mario. 1954. La población hispanoamericana y su distribución social en el siglo XVIII. *Revista de Estudios Políticos* 52 (no. 78):111–41.

———. 1958. La sociedad colonial americana en el siglo XVIII. *Historia de España y América*. Vol. 4. Ed. J. Vicens Vives. Barcelona: Editorial Vicens Vives.

Herrera Canales, Inés, Cuauhtémoc Velasco Avila, and Eduardo Flores Clair. 1981. *Etnia y clase: Los trabajadores ingleses de la Compañía Real del Monte y Pachuca, 1824–1906*. Mexico City: Departamento de investigaciones históricas, INAH (Cuaderno de trabajo, 38).

Hirschman, Albert O. 1965. *Journeys toward progress*. Garden City, N.Y.: Doubleday.

Holloway, Thomas. 1980. *Immigrants on the land: Coffee and society in São Paulo, 1886–1934*. Chapel Hill: University of North Carolina Press.

Hugarte, Renzo Pi, and Daniel Vidart. 1969. *El legado de los inmigrantes*. Vol. 2. Montevideo: Nuestra Tierra.

Humphreys, Robin A. 1946. *The evolution of modern Latin America.* London: Clarendon Press.

Ianni, Octavio. 1966. Do polonés ao polaco. *Raças e classes sociais no Brasil.* Rio de Janeiro: Civilizacão Brasileira.

IDB. 1966. *Social Progress Trust Fund: 1965 report.* Washington, D.C.: Interamerican Development Bank.

IDB. 1981. *Social Progress Trust Fund: 1980–81 report.* Washington, D.C.: Interamerican Development Bank.

International migration policies and programmes: A world survey. 1982. New York: United Nations Department of International Economic and Social Affairs. Population Studies 80.

Jacobs, Raúl. 1969. *Consecuencias sociales del alambramiento (1872–1880).* Montevideo: Ediciones de la Banda Oriental.

Kätsch, E. M., and Siegfried Kätsch. 1970. *Sosua—verheisenes Land: Eine Dokumentation zu Adaptationsproblemen deutsch-jüdischer Siedler der Dominikanischen Republik.* Dortmund: COSAL.

Kellenbenz, H. 1974. Mercanti stranieri in Brasile: Origini etnico-religiose e integrazione. *Quaderni Storici* (Ancona) 25:46–78.

Kenny, Michael. 1973. The return of the Spanish emigrant. In *Kulturvariation i Sydeuropa.* Ed. Knut Weibust. Copenhagen: NEFA.

Klein, Herbert S. 1981. La integración de inmigrantes italianos en la Argentina y los Estados Unidos: Un análisis comparativo. *Desarrollo económico* 21 (no. 31): 3–27.

Kohlhepp, Gerd. 1976. Planung und heutige Situation staatlicher kleinbäuerliche Kolonisationsprojekte an der Transamazônica. *Geographische Zeitschrift* 64 (no. 3):171–211.

————. 1980. Analysis of state and private regional development projects in the Brazilian Amazon basin. *Applied Geography and Development* 16: 53–79.

Köllmann, Wolfgang, and Peter Marschalk. 1980. German overseas emigration since 1815. *Migrations:* 447–65.

Korolev, N. V. 1976. Emigración de Rusia a América Latina a fines del siglo XIX, comienzos del siglo XX. *Jahrbuch für Geschichte von Staat, Wirtschaft und Gesellschaft Lateinamerikas* 13:31–37.

Kossok, Manfred. n.d. *Im Schatten der Heiligen Allianz: Deutschland und Lateinamerika, 1815–1830.* East Berlin: Akademie Verlag.

Kritz, Mary M. 1975. The impact of international migration on Venezuelan demographic and social structure. *International Migration Review* 9:513–43.

Kritz, Mary M., and Douglas R. Gurak, eds. 1979. International migration trends in Latin America: Research and data survey. *International Migration Review* 13 (no. 3):407–27.

Kula, Marcin. 1976. El Brasil y Polonia a fines del siglo XIX en las cartas de los campesinos emigrados. *Jahrbuch für Geschichte von Staat, Wirtschaft und Gesellschaft Lateinamerikas* 13:38–55.

————. 1983. El proletariado polaco en Cuba en el período de entre-guerras. *Capitales* 2:358–67.

Laguerre, Michel S. 1983. Haitian immigrants in the United States: A historical overview. In *White collar migrants in the Americas and the Caribbean*. Ed. Arnaud F. Marks and Hebe M. C. Vessuri. Leiden: Royal Institute of Linguistics and Anthropology.

La Riva, Juan Pérez de. 1964. Documentos para la historia de las gentes sin historia: el tráfico de culíes chinos. *Revista de la Biblioteca Nacional José Martí* (Havana) 6 (no. 2). 89.

————. 1975. La inmigración antillana en Cuba durante el primer tercio del siglo XX. *Revista de la Biblioteca Nacional José Martí (Havana) 18 (no. 2):75–87.*

Laurence, K. O. 1971. *Immigration into the West Indies in the 19th century*. St. Lawrence, Barbados: Caribbean University Press.

Lee, Everett. 1966. A theory of migration. In *Migration*. Ed. J. A. Jackson. London: Cambridge University Press.

Lee, Samuel James. 1970. *Moses of the New World: The work of Baron Hirsch*. New York: Yoseleff.

Lepkowski, Tadeusz. 1983. Pequeños empresarios judío-polacos en México. *Capitales* 2.

Lewin, Boleslao. 1971. *¿Cómo fue la inmigración judía a la Argentina?* Buenos Aires: Plan Ultra.

Liebermann, José. 1966. *Los judíos en la Argentina*. Buenos Aires: Libra.

Lier, R. A. J. van. 1971. *Frontier society: A social analysis of the history of Surinam*. The Hague: Koninklijk Institut voor Taal-, Land- en Volkenkunde.

Lindahl, Göran G. 1962. *Uruguay's new path: A study in politics during the first colegiado, 1919–33*. Stockholm: Library and Institute of Ibero-American Studies.

Lindqvist, Sven. 1973. *Jord och makt i Sydamerika*. Stockholm: Bonniers.

Linhares, Maria Yedda, and Maria Bárbaro Levy. 1973. Aspectos da história demográfica e social do Río de Janeiro (1808–1889). *L'histoire quantitative du Brésil de 1800 à 1930*. Paris: Centre National de la Recherche Scientifique: 123–38.

Livermore, Harold V. 1950. Nueva Australia. *Hispanic American Historical Review* 30:290–313.

Lockhart, James. 1968. *Spanish Peru 1532–1560: A colonial society*. Madison: University of Wisconsin Press.

————. 1972. *The men in Cajamarca: A social and biographical study of the first conquerors of Peru*. Austin: University of Texas Press.

————. 1976. *Letters and people to Spain*. Vol. 2 of *First images of America*. Ed. Fredi Chiappelli. Berkeley and Los Angeles: University of California Press: 783–96.

Lockhart, James, and Enrique Otte, eds. 1976. *Letters and people of the Spanish Indies: Sixteenth Century*. Cambridge: Cambridge University Press.

López, R. Paula. 1937. Immigration and settlement in Brazil, Argentina, and Uruguay. Pts. 1, 2. *International Labour Review* 35 (no. 1):215–46; 352–83.

López de Velasco, Juan. 1971. *Geografía y descripción universal de las Indias*. Ed. M. Jiménez de la Espada. Preliminary study by Carmen González Muñoz. Madrid: Biblioteca de Autores Españoles desde la formación del lenguaje hasta nuestros días, no. 248.

Lorenzoni, Julio. 1975. *Memorias de un inmigrante italiano*. Porto Alegre: Livraria Sulina Editora.

Lundahl, Mats. 1982. A note on Haitian migration to Cuba, 1890–1934. *Cuban Studies/Estudios cubanos* 12 (no. 2): 21–36.

Lynch, John. 1973. *The Spanish American revolutions, 1808–1926*. New York: Norton.

MacDonald, J. S. 1963–64. Agricultural organization, migration and labour militancy in rural Italy. *Economic History Review* (Utrecht) n.s. 16:61–75.

MacGaffey, Wyatt, and Clifford R. Barnett. 1962. *Twentieth-century Cuba: The background of the Castro revolution*. Garden City, N.Y.: Doubleday.

Magalhães-Godinho, Vitorino. 1974. L'émigration portugaise du XVe siècle à nos jours: Histoire d'une constante structurale. *Conjoncture économique, structure sociales: Hommage à Ernest Labrousse*. Paris and The Hague: Mouton.

Maloof, Louis J. 1959. A sociological study of Arabic-speaking people in Mexico. Ph.D. diss., University of Florida.

Mangalam, J. J., and H. K. Schwarzweller, 1968. General theory in the study of migration: Current needs and difficulties. *International Migration Review* 3 (no. 1): 3–21.

Mangalam, J. J., and H. K. Schwarzweller. 1970. Some theoretical guidelines toward a sociology of migration. *International Migration Review* 4 (no. 1):3–13.

Maram, Sheldon L. 1977. The immigrant and the Brazilian labor movement, 1890–1920. In *Essays concerning the socio-economic history of Brazil and Portuguese India*. Ed. Dauril Alden and Warren Dean. Gainesville: University Presses of Florida.

Marcílio, María Luiza. 1965. Industrialisation et mouvement ouvrier à São Paulo au début du XXe siècle. *Le mouvement social* (Paris) 53:111–29.

Marks, Arnaud F., and Hebe M. C. Vessuri, eds. 1983. *White collar migrants in the Americans and the Caribbean*. Leiden: Royal Institute of Linguistics and Anthropology.

Mármora, Lelio. 1979. Labor migration policy in Colombia. *International Migration Review* 13 (no. 3):440–54.

Marrero, Levi. 1964. *Venezuela y sus recursos: Una geografía visualizada*. Caracas: Cultural Venezolana.

Marsal, Juan Francisco. 1972. *Hacer la América: Biografía de un emigrante*. Barcelona: Ariel.

Marschalck, Peter. 1976. Social and economic conditions of European emigration to South America in the 19th and 20th centuries. *Jahrbuch für Geschichte von Staat, Wirtschaft und Gesellschaft Lateinamerikas* 13:11–30.

Marshall, Adriana. 1979. Immigrant workers in the Buenos Aires labor market. *International Migration Review* 13 (no. 3):488–501.

Marshall, Adriana, and Dora Orlansky. 1983. Inmigración de países limítrofes y demanda de mano de obra en la Argentina, 1940–1980. *Desarrollo Económico* 23 (no. 89):35–58.

Martínez Díaz, Nelson. 1978. La inmigración canaria en Uruguay durante la primera mitad del siglo XIX: Una sociedad para el transporte de colonos. *Revista de Indias* 38 (nos. 151/52):349–402.

Matterlart, Armand, and Michèle Matterlart. 1964. *La problematique du peuplement latinoaméricain*. Paris: Editeurs Universitaires.

Mazet, Claude. 1976. Population et société à Lima aux XVIᵉ et XVIIIᵉ siècles: La paroisse San Sebastian (1562–1689). *Cahiers des Amériques Latines* 13/14:51–100.

McGreevey, William. 1968. Causas de la migración interna en Colombia. In *Empleo y desempleo en Colombia*. Bogotá: Editora Universidad de los Andes.

Mecham, J. Lloyd. 1966. *Church and state in Latin America: A history of political-ecclesiastical relations*. Rev. ed. Chapel Hill: University of North Carolina Press.

Meyer, Jean. 1975. L'émigration mexicaine aux Etats-Unis. *Cahiers des Amériques latines* 12 (no. 2):255–73.

Meyer, Jean, and J. Bustamante. 1975. Influence des Etats-Unis dans les migrations mexicaines. *Cahiers des Amériques Latines* 12:255–314.

Les migrations au Mexique. 1975. *Cahiers des Amériques Latines* 12 (no. 2), special issue.

Les migrations internationales de la fin du XVIIIᵉ siècle à nos jours. 1980. Paris: Centre National de la Recherche Scientifique.

Misek, Rudolf. 1967. Origen de la emigración checoslovaca a la Argentina. *Ibero-Americana Pragensia* (Prague) 1:123–31.

Moore, Joan W., ed. 1970. *Mexican Americans*. Englewood Cliffs, N.J.: Prentice-Hall.

Morales, J. 1974. *Panorama de la migración internacional entre países latinoamericanos*. Santiago de Chile: CELADE.

Morales Vergara, Julio. 1969. Evaluation of the magnitude and structure of international migration movement in Latin America 1958/67. *International Population Conference, London 1969*. Liège: International Union for the Scientific Study of Population, 1971, 4:2606.

Mörner, Magnus, ed. 1970. *Race and class in Latin America*. New York: Columbia University Press.

———. 1976. Spanish migration to the new world prior to 1810: A report on the state of research. In *First images of America: The impact of the new world on the old*. Vol. 2. Ed. Fredi Chiappelli. Berkeley and Los Angeles: University of California Press.

———. 1978. *Perfil de la sociedad rural del Cuzco a fines de la colonia*. Lima: Universidad del Pacífico.

———. 1982a. European travelogues as sources to Latin American history from the late eighteenth century until 1870. *Revista de historia de América* 93:91–149.

————. 1982b. Massutvandring över havet. In *Vandrarsläktet människan*. Stockholm: Stiftelsen Forskning och Framsteg.

Mörner, Magnus, Julia Fawaz de Viñuela, and John D. French. 1982. Comparative approaches to Latin American history. *Latin American Research Review* 17 (no. 3):55–89.

Morse, Richard M. 1971. Trends and issues in Latin American urban research, 1965–1970. *Latin American Research Review* 6 (no. 1):3–52; 6 (no. 2):19–75.

Mosk, Sanford A. 1948. Latin America and the world economy, 1850–1914. *Inter-American Economic Affairs* 2 (no. 3):53–82.

————. 1955. The coffee economy of Guatemala, 1850–1918: Development and signs of instability. *Inter-American Economic Affairs* 9 (no. 3):6–20.

Mulhall, Michael G. 1899. *The dictionary of statistics*. 4th ed. London: Routledge.

Nadal, Jordi. 1973. *La población española (siglos XVI a XX)*. 3d ed. Barcelona: Ariel.

Nath, Dwarka. 1950. *A history of Indians in British Guiana*. London: D. Nath.

Newton, Ronald C. 1977. *German Buenos Aires, 1900–1933: Social change and cultural crisis*. Austin: University of Texas Press.

————. 1982. Indifferent sanctuary: German-speaking refugees and exiles in Argentina, 1933–1945. *Journal of Interamerican Studies and World Affairs* 24 (no. 4):395–420.

Nicoulin, Martin. 1973. *La genèse de Nova Friburgo: Emigration et colonisation suisse au Brèsil, 1817–1827*. Fribourg: Editions universitaires.

Nino de Guerrero, Raúl. 1979. *Rural to urban drift in Colombia*. Lund, Sweden: University of Lund.

Normano, J. F., and A. Gerbi. 1943. *The Japanese in South America: An introductory study with special reference to Peru*. New York: Institute for Pacific Relations.

Oddone, Juan Antonio. 1966. *La emigración europea al Río de la Plata: Motivaciones y proceso de incorporación*. Montevideo: Ediciones de la Banda Oriental.

————. 1966. *La formación del Uruguay moderno*. Buenos Aires: EUDEBA.

Odell, Peter R., and David A. Preston. 1978. *Economies and societies in Latin America: A geographical interpretation*, 2nd ed. New York: John Wiley.

Oteiza, Enrique. 1971. Emigración de profesionales, técnicos y obreros calificados argentinos a los Estados Unidos. *Desarrollo Económico* 39/40:429–54.

Otte, Enrique. 1966. Cartas privadas de Puebla del siglo XVI. *Jahrbuch für Geschichte von Staat, Wirtschaft und Gesellschaft Lateinamerikas* 3:3–87.

————. 1969. Die europäischen Siedler und die Probleme der neuen Welt. *Jahrbuch für Geschichte von Staat, Wirtschaft und Gesellschaft Lateinamerikas* 6:1–40.

Palmer, Ransford W. 1983. Emigration and the economic decline of Jamaica. In *White collar migrants in the Americas and the Caribbean*, ed. Arnaud F. Marks and Hebe M. C. Vessuri. Leiden: Royal Institute of Linguistics and Anthropology.

Parry, J. H. 1964. *The Age of the Reconnaissance*. New York: Mentor.

Paulin, Axel. 1951. *Svenska öden i Sydamerika*. Stockholm: Norstedts.

Pérez, Lisandro. 1982. Iron mining and socio-demographic change in eastern Cuba, 1884–1950. *Journal of Latin American Studies* 14 (no. 2):381–406.

Pérez de la Riva, Juan. 1964. Documentos para la historia de las gentes sin historia: El tráfico de culíes chinos. *Revista de la Biblioteca Nacional José Martí* (Havana) 6 (no. 2):77–90.

————. 1975. La inmigración antillana en Cuba durante el primer tercio del siglo XX. *Revista de la Biblioteca Nacional José Martí* (Havana) 17 (no. 2):75–87.

Petrucelli, José Luis. 1979. Consequences of Uruguayan emigration: Research note. *International Migration Review* 13 (no. 3):519–26.

Les phénomènes de "frontière" dans les pays tropicaux. 1981. Paris: Centre de recherche et documentation sur l'Amérique latine.

Piel, Juan. 1974. L'importation de main-d'ouvre chinoise et le développement agricole au Pérou au XIXème siècle. *Cahiers des Amériques Latines* (Paris) 9/10:87–103.

Pike, Frederick B. 1971. Hispanismo and the non-revolutionary Spanish immigrant in Spanish America, 1900–1930. *Inter-American Economic Affairs* 25:3–30.

Pilatti Balhana, Altiva, Brasil Pinheiro Machado, and Cecilia María Westphalen. 1969. alguns aspectos relativos aõs estudos de inmigração e colonização. In *Colonização e migração: Trabalhos apresentados ao IV. simpósio dos professores universitários de história.* Ed. Eurípides Simões de Paula. São Paulo: Universidad de São Paulo.

Platt, D. C. M. 1964, 1965. British agricultural colonization in Latin America. *Inter-American Economic Affairs* 18 (no. 3):3–38; 19 (no. 1):23–42.

————. 1972. *Latin America and British trade, 1806–1914.* London: Black.

Polisensky, J. 1976. La emigración checoslovaca a América Latina 1640–1945: Problemas y fuentes. *Jahrbuch für Geschichte von Staat, Wirtschaft und Gesellschaft Lateinamerikas* 13:216–38.

Poppino, Rollie E. 1968. *Brazil: The land and people.* New York: Oxford University Press.

Portes, Alejandro, and John Walton. 1976. *Urban Latin America: The political condition from above and below.* Austin: University of Texas Press.

Presedo, Vicente Vázquez. 1971. The role of Italian migration in the development of the Argentine economy, 1875–1914. *Economía Internazionale, Rivista dell'Instituto di Economía Internazionale* (Genoa) 24:606–26.

Preston, David A., Gerardo Taveras, and Rosemary A. Preston. 1981. Emigración rural y desarrollo agrícola en la Sierra Ecuatoriana. *Revista Geográfica* 93:7–35.

Price, P., and H. Price. 1952. Demographic aspects of the Polish migration to Brazil. *Inter-American Economic Affairs* 5 (no. 4):46–58.

Quintas, Amaro. 1967. *O sentido social da Revolução Praieira.* São Paulo: Civilização Brasileira.

Recchini de Lattes, Zulima. 1969. *Migraciones en la Argentina: Estudio de las migraciones internas e internacionales, basado en datos censales 1869–1960.* Buenos Aires: Instituto Torcuato di Tella.

————. 1971. *La población de Buenos Aires: Componentes demográficos del crecimiento entre 1855 y 1960.* Buenos Aires: Instituto Torcuato di Tella.

Reed, Nelson. 1964. *The caste wars of Yucatán.* Stanford, Calif.: Stanford University Press.

Reichert, John, and Douglas S. Massey. 1980. History and trends in United States bound migration from a Mexican town. *International Migration Review* 14 (no. 4):475–91.

Reisler, Mark. 1976. *By the sweat of their brow: Mexican immigrant labor in the U.S., 1900–40.* Westport, Conn.: Greenwood Press.

Revert, Eugène. 1949. *La Martinique: Etude geographique et humaine.* Paris: L'union française.

Rial, Juan. 1980. Estadísticas históricas de Uruguay 1850–1930. Montevideo: Centro de informaciones y estudios del Uruguay. Mimeographed.

Roberts, George W. 1963. The demographic position of the Caribbean. Washington: U.S. House of Representatives Committee on the Judiciary. Subcommittee no. 1:104–06. (Study of population and immigration problems. Western Hemisphere 2:1.)

Roberts, George W., and J. Byrne. 1966–67. Summary statistics on indenture and associated migration affecting the West Indies, 1834–1918. *Population Studies* 20:125–34.

Roberts, George W., and M. A. Johnson. 1974. Factors involved in immigration and movements in the working force of British Guiana in the 19th century. *Social and Economic Studies* Jamaica) 23 (no. 1):69–83.

Rocha Nogueira, Arlinda. 1973. *A inmigracão japonesa para a lavoura cafereira paulista (1908–1922).* São Paulo: Universidade de São Paulo.

Roche, Jean. 1959. *La colonisation allemande et le Rio Grande do Sul.* Paris: Institut des hautes études de l'Amérique latine.

Rockett, Ian R. H. 1976. Immigration legislation and the flow of specialized human capital from South America to the United States. *International Migration Review* 10 (no. 3): 47–61.

Rodríguez Campos, Manuel. 1983. La inmigración canaria en los primeros años de la República venezolana. *Tierra Firme: Revista de historia y ciencias sociales* 1 (no. 1):23–34.

Rodríguez Plata, Horacio. 1968. *La inmigración alemana al estado soberano de Santander en el siglo XIX: Repercusiones socio-económicas de un proceso de transculturación.* Bogotá: Ediciones Kelly.

Rodríguez Vicente, María E. 1968. Los extranjeros y el mar en el Perú (fines del siglo XVI y comienzos del XVIII). *Anuario de Estudios Americanos* (Seville) 25:619–29.

Rogberg, Martin. 1954. *Svenskar i Latinamerika: Pionjäröden och nutida insatser.* Orebro: Lindqvists förlag.

Rogers, Andrei. 1982. Sources of urban population growth and urbanization, 1950–2000: A demographic accounting. *Economic Development and Cultural Change* 30 (no. 3):483–506.

Rogg, Eleonor Meyer. 1974. *The assimilation of Cuban exiles: The role of community and class.* New York: Aberdeen Press.

Rollo, Andrew F. 1965. *The lost cause: The confederate exodus to Mexico.* Norman: University of Oklahoma Press.

Romo, Ricardo. 1983. *East Los Angeles: History of a barrio.* Austin: University of Texas Press.

RS: Imigração e colonização. 1980. Porto Alegre: Mercado Aberto.

Rubio Mañé, J. Ignacio. 1945. Extranjeros en Mérida y Campeche. *Memorias de la Academia Mexicana de Historia* 4:3.

─────. 1966. *Gente de España en la cuidad de México: Año de 1689.* México: Archivo General de la Nación.

Safford, Frank. 1972. In search of the practical: Colombian students in foreign lands, 1845–1890. *Hispanic-American Historical Review* 52 (no. 2):230–49.

Saito, Hiroshi. 1961. *O japonês no Brasil: Estudo de mobilidade e fixação.* São Paulo: Ediciones Sociología e Política.

Samora, Julián. 1971. *Los mojados: The wetback story.* Notre Dame, Ind: University of Notre Dame Press.

Sánchez-Albornoz, Nicolás. 1974. *The population of Latin America: A history.* Berkeley and Los Angeles: University of California Press.

─────. 1982. Migración urbana y trabajo: Los indios de Arequipa, 1571–1645. *De historia e historiadores: Homenaje a José Luis Romero.* Mexico City: Siglo XXI:259–81.

Sassen-Koob, Saskia. 1979. Economic growth and immigration in Venezuela. *International Migration Review* 13 (no. 3):455–74.

Sbarra, Noel H. 1955. *Historia del alambrado en la Argentina.* Buenos Aires: Raigal.

Scarzanella, Eugenia. 1981. L'industria argentina e gli immigrati italiani: nascita della borghesia industriale bonaerense. *Annali della Fondazione Luigi Einaudi* 15: 365–412.

Schmitt, Peter A. 1963. *Paraguay und Europa: Die diplomatischen Beziehungen unter Carlos Antonio López und Francisco Solano López, 1841–1870.* West Berlin: Colloquium Verlag.

Schopflocher, Roberto. 1955. *Historia de la colonización agrícola en Argentina.* Buenos Aires: Raigal.

Schramm, Percy Ernst. 1964. Die deutsche Siedlungskolonie Dona Francisca (Brasilien: St. Catharina) im Rahmen gleichzeitiger Projekte und Verhandlungen. *Jahrbuch für Geschichte von Staat, Wirtschaft und Gesellschaft Lateinamerikas.* Cologne: Böhlau. 1:283–324.

Schuler, Monica. 1980. *"Alas, alas, Kongo": A social history of indentured African immigration into Jamaica, 1841–1865.* Baltimore: Johns Hopkins University Press.

Schwartz, Ernst, and Johan C. TeVelde. 1939. Jewish agricultural settlement in Argentina: The ICA experiment. *Hispanic-American Historical Review* 29 (no. 2):185–203.

Scobie, James R. 1964. *Revolution on the pampas: A social history of Argentine wheat 1860–1910.* Austin: University of Texas Press.

─────. 1971. *Argentina: A city and a nation.* 2d ed. New York: Oxford University Press.

————. 1974. *Buenos Aires: Plaza to suburb, 1870–1910.* New York: Oxford University Press.

Un secolo di emigrazione italiana (1876–1976). 1980. Ed. Francesco Balletta, Anna Maria Birindelli, and Franco Cerase. Rome: Centro Studi Emigrazione.

Seed, Patricia. 1982. Social dimensions of race: Mexico City, 1753. *Hispanic American Historical Review* 62 (no. 4):569–606.

Segall, Marcelo. 1972. En Amérique Latine: Développement du mouvement ouvrier et proscription. *International Review of Social History* (Amsterdam) 17:325–69.

Seraile, William. 1978. Afro-American emigration to Haiti during the civil war. *The Americas* 35 (no. 2):185–200.

Serrão, Joel. 1974. *A emigração portuguesa: Sondagem histórica.* Lisbon: Livros Horizonte.

Serrão, Joel, and Arnaldo Pereira. 1979. Inventariação das fontes e bibliografía relativas á emigração portuguesa. In *La emigración europea a la América Latina: Fuentes y estado de investigación: Informes presentados a la IV Reunión de Historiadores Latino-americanistas Europeos.* West Berlin: Colloquium Verlag.

Servin, Manuel P., ed. 1970. *The Mexican Americans: An awakening minority.* Beverly Hills, Calif.: Glencoe Press.

Simmons, Alan, and Ramiro Cardona. 1972. Rural-urban migration: Who comes, who stays, who returns? The case of Bogotá, Colombia, 1929–1968. *International Migration Review* 6 (no. 2):166–81.

Simon, Fanny S. 1946. Anarchism and anarcho-syndicalism in South America. *Hispanic American Historical Review* 26 (no. 1):38–59.

Sims, Harold D. 1971. Las clases económicas y la dicotomía criollo-peninsular en Durango, 1827. *Historia Mexicana* 20 (no. 4):539–62.

————. 1972. Japanese postwar migration to Brazil: An analysis of data presently available. *International Migration Review* 6 (no. 3):246–66.

————. 1974a. Japanese agriculturalists in Brazil and Paraguay: A review of the literature. *Peasant Studies Newsletter* 3 (no. 2):13-19.

————. 1974b. *La expulsión de los españoles de Mexico (1821–1828).* Mexico City: Fondo de Cultura Económica.

————. 1982a. *La descolonización de México: Los conflictos entre mexicanos y españoles (1821–1831).* Mexico City: Fondo de Cultura Económica.

————. 1982b. Los españoles exiliados de México en 1829. *Historia Mexicana* 3 (no. 3):391–414.

————. 1985. *La reconquista de México: La historia de los atentados españoles (1821–1830).* Mexico City: Fondo de Cultura Económica.

Sindico, Domenico E. 1983. Inmigración europea y desarrollo industrial: El caso de Monterrey, México. *Capitales* 2:436–67.

Sjöstrand, María E. Castellano de. 1975. La población de Venezuela: Migraciones internas y distribución espacial, 1908–1935. *Semestre Hispánico* (Caracas) 1 (no. 5):62.

Skidmore, Thomas E. 1979. Workers and soldiers: Urban labor movements and elite responses in twentieth-century Latin America. In *Elites, Masses and modernization in Latin America, 1850–1930*. Austin: University of Texas Press, 1979.

Slicher van Bath, B. H. 1976. Desarrollo agrícola en Europa entre 1800 y 1914. *Jahrbuch für Geschichte von Staat, Wirtschaft und Gesellschaft Lateinamerikas* 13:11–30.

Smith, Lois Elwyn. 1955. *Mexico and the Spanish republicans*. Berkeley and Los Angeles: University of California Press.

Smolana, Krzysztof. 1983. Los obreros, empresarios y capitales polacos en el proceso de industrialización y de sindicalización de América Latina. *Capitales* 1:102–24.

Socolow, Susan Migden. 1978. *The merchants of Buenos Aires, 1778–1810. Family and commerce*. Cambridge: Cambridge University Press.

Sofer, Eugene F. 1976. Immigration and entrepreneurship in Buenos Aires, 1890–1927: The Jewish case. Presented at the meeting of the Pacific Coast Council on Latin American Studies, Tempe, Arizona.

Solari, Aldo E. 1958. *Sociología rural nacional*. 2d ed. Montevideo: Facultad de Derecho, 1958.

Solberg, Carl. 1970. *Immigration and nationalism: Argentina and Chile, 1890–1914*. Austin: University of Texas Press.

———. 1982. Peopling the prairies and the pampas: The impact of immigration on Argentina and Canadian development, 1870–1930. *Journal of Inter-American Studies and World Affairs* 24 (no. 2):131–61.

Spalding, Hobart A., Jr., comp. 1970. *La clase trabajadora argentina (documentos para su historia, 1890–1912)*. Buenos Aires: Editorial Galerna.

———. 1977. *Organized labor in Latin America: Historical case studies of workers in dependent societies*. New York: New York University Press.

———. 1983. Capitales, empresarios y obreros europeos en los procesos de industrialización y sindicalización en América Latina, 1850–1930: Una breve síntesis. *Capitales* 1:209–35.

Stang, Gudmund. 1976. La emigración escandinava a la América Latina, 1800–1940. *Jahrbuch für Geschichte von Staat, Wirtschaft und Gesellschaft Lateinamerikas* 13:293–330.

———. 1983. Aspectos de la política de personal de las empresas británicas en América Latina, 1880–1930. *Capitales* 2.

Statistical abstract of Latin America. 1967, 1980. Los Angeles: University of California at Los Angeles, Latin American Center.

Stenbäck, Karin. 1973. *Utvandringen från Sverige till Brasilien 1868–1891. Tre studier*. M.A. thesis, Institute of History, University of Uppsala.

Stewart, Watt. 1951. *Chinese bondage in Peru: A history of the Chinese coolie in Peru, 1840–1874*. Chapel Hill: University of North Carolina Press.

Stols, Eddy. 1973. O mercaderes flamengos em Portugal e no Brasil antes das conquistas holandesas. *Anáis de História* (São Paulo) 5:9–54.

———. 1976. Penetração económica, assistência técnica e "brain drain". Aspectos da emigração belga para a América Latina por volta de 1900. *Jahrbuch für Geschichte von Staat, Wirtschaft und Gesellschaft Lateinamerikas* 13:361–85.

―――. 1979. L'expansion belge en Amerique Latine vers 1900. *Academie Royale des Sciences d'Outre-Mer: Bulletin des Seances 2.*

Strelco, Andrei. 1975. Primeros inmigrantes ucrainos en Latinoamérica. *América Latina* (Moscow) 1:89–98.

Suárez, Santiago-Gerardo. 1975. *Inmigración y naturalización.* Caracas: S.R.L.

Szuchman, Mark D. 1977. The limits of the melting pot in urban Argentina: Marriage and integration in Córdoba, 1869–1909. *Hispanic American Historical Review* 57 (no. 1):24–50.

―――. 1980. *Mobility and integration in urban Argentina. Córdoba in the Liberal era.* Austin: University of Texas Press.

Thistlethwaite, Frank. 1960. Migration from Europe overseas in the nineteenth and twentieth centuries. *XI. Congrés International des Sciences Historique: Rapports* (Uppsala) 5:32–60.

Thomas, Brinley. 1954. *Migration and economic growth: A study of Great Britain and the Atlantic economy.* Cambridge: Cambridge University Press.

Thomas, Hugh. 1971. *Cuba: The pursuit of freedom.* New York: Harper & Row.

Thomas, Mary Elizabeth. 1974. *Jamaica and the voluntary laborers from Africa, 1840–1865.* Gainesville: The University Presses of Florida.

Tigner, James L. 1961. Shindo Remmei: Japanese nationalism in Brazil. *Hispanic American Historical Review* 40:515–32.

―――. 1963. The Ryukyuans in Bolivia. *Hispanic American Historical Review* 43:206–29.

―――. 1978. The Ryukyans in Peru, 1906–1952. *The Americas* 35 (no. 1):20–44.

―――. 1982. Japanese settlement in eastern Bolivia and Brazil. *Journal of Inter-American Studies and World Affairs* 24 (no. 4):496–517.

Tobler, Hans Werner. 1979. Emigración europea a América Latina, Suiza. In *La emigración europea a la américa Latina: Fuentes y estado de investigación: Informes presentados a la IVª Reunión de Historiadores Latinoamericanistas Europeos.* West Berlin: Colloquium Verlag.

Torrado, Susana. 1979. International migration policies in Latin America. *International Migration Review* 13 (no. 3):428–39.

Trends and characteristics of international migration since 1950. 1979. New York: United Nations Department of Economic and Social Affairs. Demographic Studies 64.

Tsung likokuo shihwuyamen. [1876] 1970. *Report of the commission sent by China to ascertain the condition of Chinese coolies in Cuba.* Reprint. Taipei: Ch'eng Wen Publishing Co.

Ugalde, Antonio, F. D. Bean, and Gilberto Cárdenas. 1979. International migration from the Dominican Republic: Findings from a national survey. *International Migration Review* 13 (no. 2):235–54.

UN. 1979. *Trends and characteristics of international migration since 1950.* New

York: United Nations Department of Economic and Social Affairs. Demographic Studies 64.

UN. 1982a. *International migration policies and programmes: A world survey*. New York: United Nations Department of International Economic and Social Affairs. Population Studies 80.

UN. 1982b. *World population trends and policies: 1981 monitoring report*. New York: United Nations Department of Social and Economic Affairs. Population Trends 1.

Valdés, Nelson P., and Edwin Lieuwen. 1971. *The Cuban revolution: A research-study guide (1959–1969)*. Albuquerque: University of Mexico Press.

Varga, Hernando. 1979. A 1,000,000 move: Migration from Colombia to Venezuela. *Migration Today* 26:21–22.

Varga, Ilona. 1976. A kivándorlás irányváltozása és a magyar kivándorl beilleszkedése Latin-Amerikában a két világháború között. *Acta Historica* 56. (Deals with Hungarian migration and assimilation in Latin America in the 1920s and 1930s. Summary in Spanish.)

Vázquez-Presedo, Vicente. 1971. The role of Italian migration in the development of the Argentine economy, 1875–1914. *Economía Internazionale: Rivista dell'Istituto di Economía Internazionale* (Genoa) 24:606–26.

Viega, Danielo. 1981. Socioeconomic structure and population displacements: The Uruguayan case. *Canadian Journal of Latin American Studies*, n.s. 6 (no. 12): 1–25.

Vieytes, A. 1969. La emigración salvadoreña a Honduras. *Estudios Centroamericanos* 254/55:399–406.

Wachowicz, Ruy Christovam. 1976. *Abranches: Un estudio de história demográfica*. Curitiba: Editora Gráfica Vicentina.

Waibel, Leo. 1955. *Die europäische Kolonisation Südbrasiliens*. Bonn: Colloquium Geographicum.

Weibust, Knut, ed. 1973. *Kulturvariation i Sydeuropa*. Copenhagen: NEFA.

Weisbrot, Robert. 1979. *The Jews of Argentina from the Inquisition to Perón*. Philadelphia: Jewish Publication Society of America.

Weller, Judith Ann. 1968. *The East Indian indenture in Trinidad*. Río Piedras, Puerto Rico: Institute of Caribbean Studies.

Wilkie, James W. 1970. La ciudad de México como imán de la población económicamente activa, 1930–1965. In *Historia y sociedad en el mundo de habla española: Homenaje a José Miranda*. Ed. Bernardo García Martínez. Mexico City: El Colegio de México:381–95.

Willems, Emílio. 1946. *A aculturação dos alemães no Brasil*. São Paulo: Civilização Brasileira.

———. 1958. Minority subcultures in Brazil. *Miscellanea Paul Rivet*. Vol. 2. Mexico City: UNAM.

Williams, Glyn. 1975. *The desert and the dream. A study of Welsh colonization in Chubut, 1865–1915*. Cardiff: University of Wales Press.

———. 1976. La emigración galesa en la Patagonia, 1865–1915. *Jahrbuch für Geschichte von Staat, Wirtschaft and Gesellschaft Lateinamerikas* 13:239–92.

Williams-Bailey, W., and P. H. Pemberton. 1972. *Nelson's West Indian geography: A new study of the Commonwealth Caribbean and Guayana.* London: Thomas Nelson and Sons.

Wiznitzer, Arnold. 1960. *Jews in Colonial Brazil.* New York: Columbia University Press.

Wolf, Eric R. 1982. *Europe and the people without history.* Berkeley and Los Angeles: University of California Press.

Wolff, Inge. 1961. *Zur Geschichte der Ausländer im Spanischen Amerika.* In *Europe and Übersee: Festchrift für Egmont Zechlin.* Hamburg: Verlag Hans-Bredow-Institut:78–108.

Wood, Charles H. 1982. Equilibrium and historical-structural perspectives on migration. *International Migration Review* 16 (no.2):298–319.

Wood, Donald. 1968. *Trinidad in transition: The years after slavery.* New York: Oxford University Press.

World population trends and policies: 1981 monitoring report. 1982. New York: United Nations Department of Social and Economic Affiars. Population Trends 1.

Worrall, Janet E. 1972. Italian immigration to Peru: 1860–1914. Ph.D. diss., Indiana University, Bloomington.

Young, George F. W. 1974. *The Germans in Chile: Immigration and colonization, 1849–1914.* New York: Center for Migration Studies.

Zaragoza Ruvira, Gonzalo. 1972. Enrico Malatesta y el anarquismo argentino. *Historiografía e bibliografía americanistas* 16 (no. 3):401–24.

Zuccarini, Emilio. 1910. *I lavori degli Italiani nella Republica Argentina.* Buenos Aires: Compañia general de fósforos, 1909.

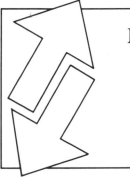

Index

173

PITT LATIN AMERICAN SERIES

Cole Blasier, Editor

ARGENTINA

Argentina in the Twentieth Century
David Rock, Editor

Discreet Partners: Argentina and the USSR Since 1917
Aldo César Vacs

Juan Perón and the Reshaping of Argentina
Frederick C. Turner and José Enrique Miguens, Editors

BRAZIL

The Politics of Social Security in Brazil
James M. Malloy

Urban Politics in Brazil: The Rise of Populism, 1925–1945
Michael L. Conniff

COLOMBIA

Gaitán of Colombia: A Political Biography
Richard E. Sharpless

Roads to Reason: Transportation, Administration, and Rationality in Colombia
Richard E. Hartwig

CUBA

Army Politics in Cuba, 1898–1958
Louis A. Pérez, Jr.

Cuba Between Empires. 1878–1902
Louis A. Pérez, Jr.

Cuba, Castro, and the United States
Philip W. Bonsal

Cuba in the World
Cole Blasier and Carmelo Mesa-Lago, Editors

Intervention, Revolution, and Politics in Cuba, 1913–1921
Louis A. Pérez, Jr.

Revolutionary Change in Cuba
Carmelo Mesa-Lago, Editor

The United States and Cuba: Hegemony and Dependent Development, 1880–1934
Jules Robert Benjamin

MEXICO

Essays on Mexican Kinship
Hugo G. Nutini, Pedro Carrasco, and James M. Taggart, Editors

The Politics of Mexican Oil
George W. Grayson

US POLICIES

Cuba, Castro, and the United States
Philip W. Bonsal

The Hovering Giant: U.S. Responses to Revolutionary Change in Latin America
Cole Blasier

Illusions of Conflict: Anglo-American Diplomacy Toward Latin America
Joseph Smith

Puerto Rico and the United States, 1917–1933
Truman R. Clark

The United States and Cuba: Hegemony and Dependent Development, 1880–1934
Jules Robert Benjamin

USSR POLICIES

Discreet Partners: Argentina and the USSR Since 1917
Aldo César Vacs

The Giant's Rival: The USSR and Latin America
Cole Blasier

OTHER NATIONAL STUDIES

Barrios in Arms: Revolution in Santo Domingo
José A. Moreno

Beyond the Revolution: Bolivia Since 1952
James M. Malloy and Richard S. Thorn, Editors

Black Labor on a White Canal: Panama, 1904–1981
Michael L. Conniff

The Origins of the Peruvian Labor Movement, 1883–1919
Peter Blanchard

The Overthrow of Allende and the Politics of Chile, 1964–1976
Paul E. Sigmund

Panajachel: A Guatemalan Town in Thirty-Year Perspective
Robert E. Hinshaw

Rebirth of the Paraguayan Republic: The First Colorado Era, 1878–1904
Harris G. Warren

SOCIAL SECURITY

The Politics of Social Security in Brazil
James M. Malloy

Social Security in Latin America: Pressure Groups, Stratification, and Inequality
Carmelo Mesa-Lago

OTHER STUDIES

Adventurers and Proletarians: The Story of Migrants in Latin America
Magnus Mörner, with the collaboration of Harold Sims

Authoritarianism and Corporatism in Latin America
James M. Malloy, Editor

Constructive Change in Latin America
Cole Blasier, Editor

Female and Male in Latin America: Essays
Ann Pescatello, Editor

Public Policy in Latin America: A Comparative Survey
John W. Sloan

Selected Latin American One-Act Plays
Francesco Colecchia and Julio Matas, Editors and Translators

The State and Capital Accumulation in Latin America: Brazil, Chile, Mexico
Christian Anglade and Carlos Fortin, Editors